A POTTERIES LAD

Stanley W. Swain

Overleaf:

An artistic view of Burslem C 1914, from St. Margaret's church Porthill where my parents are buried.

Left hand photo: A winter scene of St. Paul's church (later demolished due to foundation problems thought to be caused by subsidence by mining), with Lower Hall Street on the left.

Right hand photo: Brothers Swain – Stanley (November 17 1915), Austin, (November 23 1920) – Vallance (November 24 1925).

Front cover illustration by the author,
Coloured by Derek Potter

Also: 'I SURVIVED' ISBN 0 9523501 0 6

A POTTERIES LAD

Stanley W Swain

To Sheila,

With my Best Wishes
for another Birthday

Stanley.

October 2003.

First published in Great Britain
By Stanley W Swain
The Sheiling
5 Denmark Rise
Diss
Norfolk IP22 4LG
2003

ISBN 9523501 1 4

Design, artwork and
produced in England by
COPYDISS
St Nicholas Street
Diss
Norfolk IP22 4LB

----------------- CONTENTS -------------------

ACKNOWLEDGEMENTS

I am indebted to Arthur Holt and Milly Bloor who introduced me to old copies of The Staffordshire Sentinel's Special Supplement, 'The Way We Were'. Having left Burslem over sixty years ago the pictures reminded me of my child and teenage years which stimulated me to record those times. My thanks also to Carmel Dennison for her book 'Burslem People and Building' which added to my interest. My appreciation becoming a member of the Arnold Bennett Society also to other people who contributed pictures and Marjorie Smith's and Isobel Lawton's proof reading.

DEDICATION

To the fond memory of my parents, Mother's loving care and Father's strict but understanding discipline. Who after his death I discovered he had kept notes of my career in his diaries.   Also to my late wife Grace, whose love, help and encouragement with live wire daughter Elaine's assistance.

BURSLEM TOWN

This unique aerial picture of Burslem suggests it was taken during the summer holidays (Wakes Week), when all the Pot-banks were shut down because not a wisp of smoke is to be seen.

(My thanks to Donald Morris for the picture)

CHAPTER ONE

THE EARLY YEARS.

My earliest days, not remembered by me but often recounted by my parents to friends, was, as a month old baby, I was carried down into the cellar when a German Zeppelin was over Tunstall. A picture in The Evening Sentinel's Special Supplement, Number 14, showed a picture of a zeppelin with the text recording it passing over Tunstall, dropping a bomb at Chesterton. Whether this was the same incident one cannot be sure but as I was born November 1915 and the date in the Supplement, 1917, the picture in daylight, it was probably another occasion.

However, the incident in which I was the 'Star' was during the night because my father was carrying me with mother following with a lighted candlestick downstairs to the cellar. Steps led down from ground floor but at the bottom step one had to turn left-handed into the cellar where the headroom was low. Father had successfully negotiated the pantry shelves at the top but bumped my head when entering the cellar which not only awakened me but I lustily gave vent to being so rudely introduced with pain to a cold, dark and unfamiliar place! My screams must have reverberated round the dark empty cellar shown in the flickering candle light and my Mother, already under some tension, criticised my Father severely, not only because he had injured her precious child, and with a scream, "Now you've cone it, those Germans up there will hear him and come to bomb us!"

The lights of Tunstall (about a mile and a half away) could be seen over the green fields from the back bedroom of our home in Hall Street, so the proximity of that night's activity by the airship was very much on our 'Home Ground'! I vaguely remember some talk about two houses being bomb damaged in Tunstall but I'm not sure of its authenticity.

Another baby incident recounted by my parents was as a month old baby, asserting my male presence for the attention of my Mother during the night. From my cot with the side down adjacent to my parents' bed (Mother's side), I would cry until taking my place between them comforted me. At some point in time Dad decided that he was not prepared to put up with this noisy intrusion any longer, so I was removed from Mother's arms and placed firmly at the foot of their bed on top of a cold eiderdown, and advised that I would stay there until I stopped 'Blarting' – crying. I was never told how long I was out in the 'wilderness' but from that night on peace reigned supreme and once in my cot was very happy to stay there the whole night through.

Another baby habit I had was sucking my thumb. I do remember how sweet it tasted and apparently persisted in the comforting ritual for a long time until Mother began to worry, often trying to break me of the habit. She did try putting Bitter Alum on it but that failed because I used to get Rip, the dog, to lick it off so that I could continue. Father used to say when Mother tried to stop the dog licking scabs on our legs, "Don't worry dogs saliva has a healing effect like disinfectant". However, getting it direct from my thumb may have contributed to me reaching four score years plus!

Our home in Hall Street was the centre one of a group of seven, at the bottom near the church (later demolished due to becoming unsafe from subsidence). It had three upstairs bedrooms, a 'living' room with kitchen range and as the name implies, where most of the domestic activities occurred. A back kitchen, with sink and a coal fired boiler, called 'The Copper' (presumably a name from the early ones: our's was made of cast iron and the watch-word was to never let it boil dry because it will crack). It was in an alcove with a vent, very necessary during Mother's washday! The kitchen, her main workshop, also contained a gas ring, used for frying and boiling hot water when the wash-boiler's fire was giving trouble or making a bowl of starch with a dash of blue to stiffen Father's and our 'best' shirts.

102 HALL STREET

The green painted house, in the front bedroom was my birthplace. St Paul's churchyard gate and wall, minus iron gates and railing, where the horse and cart crashed, left centre.

The front room (Parlour or Best room) was only used for entertaining visitors, mostly on Sundays, which invariably included singing around the piano played by Father. Coal fires provided the heating with grates in the bedrooms and coal gas mantled fittings in all rooms in the centre of the ceiling, but in the main bedroom on the chimneybreast. Fires or gaslights upstairs were seldom used but I remember well the November periods when my brothers were born and seeing Mother's in her warm cosily lit bedroom. Candlesticks provided the flickering illumination when retiring to bed and an acquired skill to extinguish them with a wet thumb and forefinger to avoid the smell from a smouldering wick.

An outside toilet at the bottom of the yard was the only sanitation; chamber pots 'gusunders' and a commode for Mother were used for 'action' during the night. A shared refuse house between ours and a neighbour's toilet was emptied, not too frequently, and in the summer used to be a bit smelly from the mixture of ashes, tins and rotten food, well past their sell-by date!

Another view of Hall Street, with our Mark II 1966
Humber Sceptre in the foreground

Another reminiscence of my baby years was a small swing which hung from the ceiling in the living room. I remember it being used by my brother Austin five years younger than me. It was made by my father with ropes threaded through bamboo tubes held apart with wooden distant pieces to form a square box; legs threaded through with ample freedom but comfortably captivated us. It was suspended from the ceiling about four feet from the floor, over the sewing machine, in front of the window thereby keeping us amused by outside activities and removed from the danger of being trodden on during the crawling stage. The view from the window was much impaired during latter years when the field behind our home was filled with rubbish from the Pottery Works (called Shaudrucks) upon which houses were later built, completely blocking the view.

I have little memory of my first years spent at school (babies class), but I do recall that we were taught the alphabet from pictures. e.g. T being an umbrella and N M, showing one and two cow sheds, and taught to pronounce them phonetically.

Later when I was allowed to explore beyond the back yard gate, I used to visit a neighbour, who taught me some Potteries slang expressions to quote to my mother on my return. He knew my mother would be upset because she being a Londoner did not want her son to be vulgar, particularly in his speech. She and my father must have suffered a cultural shock when they began their married life in Porthill, shortly to move from rented accommodation to their own house in Burslem. Both were 'foreigners' having spent their formative years, mother in Camberwell and my father in Newark, Nottinghamshire.

I well recall mother telling us how she was repeatedly asked by the shopkeepers what she wanted, just to hear her 'foreign' accent! Like most folk I've met from South of the Wash she thought she had no accent, as does my wife, who also was born in the metropolis of London. I think accents were more pronounced during my childhood, indeed at school we could tell which neighbourhood our school mates came from because there were slight differences in their speech.

The walk to Hill Top School was literally true in my case because where I lived was near the bottom of Hall Street and the school at the top. Hall Street was short but with a very steep gradient which made it difficult for horse-drawn carts, car and lorries gradually replaced them in later years. On the downhill side of the road, a track of smooth flagstones with rough set-stones in between provided the heavily laden drays and carts to travel safely downwards. One or two wheels were chained onto a steel slipper shoe allowing the locked wheels to slide in dry weather, causing sparks to fly from the flagstones, and the horses to dig their heavily shod hooves into the sets to apply their weight as an additional braking force. On one occasion, which fortunately I did not see, a cart did get out of control, I think a slipper chain broke and the cart crashed at the bottom against the church boundary wall with its iron railing. The cart smashed and, most distressing, the horse severely injured. The upward climb taxed the horse's power and skill of the drivers but was safer; a zigzag course up the hill, sometimes with two horses with rests when the driver judged that their stamina was at its limit. A critical decision because gaining momentum again after a halt was difficult with a heavily laden vehicle in a narrow road.

Horses were well cared for and in many cases a firm understanding existed between them and their drivers. As in all walks of life a minority who were cruel to their dumb animals, disgrace the majority. I shall always remember an occasion when a drunken owner staggered from a pub at the top of Hall Street in Liverpool Road, and started kicking and punching his poor emaciated horse because it refused to move. I was returning to school with a pal after lunch and we both shouted at him but to no avail, but not to be late for school we had to hurry away. We were both very disturbed and unhappy, even today I could identify the man if shown a picture of him! I found out where he lived and was further shocked by the condition of his house and hovel where the horse was kept.

Nearly all the householders requirements were delivered by horse-drawn vehicles, bread, milk daily and I well remember the wonderful smell of newly baked bread when the man opened the van door, also the extra slop of milk into our jug after the correct measure had been put in by the milkman.

A recent suggestion (probably by a university person) that horses should be provided with napkins at a seaside town because complaints had been made about the horse manure being a nuisance and possibly a health risk along the promenade, reminded me of Mother's call "Gold Dust". A cry which we children answered by a quick dash into the street with small shovel and bucket to collect the freshly deposited manure, to be used on our small front garden or later taken to Dad's allotment. Speed being essential before a neighbour gathered the much sort after deposit!

Sanitary needs for horse and driver were taken for granted when on the public highway, as I believe a driver was legally allowed to urinate on the offside wheel of his cart if and when necessary. A very sensible law, thus he was able to hold the reins and control the horse, should it be startled by an unusual sound or sight. It was not uncommon to see the horse accompany it's master when it heard the water music behind, thus providing a pleasant duet for all to see and appreciate! On one occasion, I remember asking a driver why hessian sacks were draped along both shafts of his cart. "Ahr lad, he's a full blooded stallion and should a mare, in season, be approaching he likes to show his credentials which some members of the public seeing, may be embarrassed or envious, so I provide him with a courtesy skirt". When I asked what 'in season' meant, he said "You'd better ask yer fayther, I mun get on".

Burslem and most districts in Stoke-on-Trent were hilly areas which provided good strenuous walking exercise with changing views when one could see between the smoke clouds. The pottery Works (Potbanks) were family concerns and there were many mostly situated among the streets of houses, their bottlenecked ovens only feet above the rooftops. Streets near the kilns, on the four to five firing days were subjected to large volumes of black smoke depending on wind direction. Women used to try to be informed on the firing programmes so that washing lines were strategically placed to avoid disastrous results.

Air pollution was an accepted part of living and I think only caused annoyance with the womenfolk because curtains and many household articles had to be washed frequently. Our bedroom windows were always opened at the top (sash windows), throughout the year and to mitigate draughts, Mother had pieces of fine net cloth covering the opening which had to be washed sometimes every fortnight! The practice of open bedroom windows was consolidated, when one morning an overpowering smell of gas (coal gas) was noticed upon entering the downstairs rooms. Doors and windows were hurriedly opened. I can't remember the source but my parents were convinced that the open windows had most likely saved the family from asphyxiation! To this day I always ensure some upstairs ventilation is provided.

Within two years new red brick houses changed to a dark brown getting darker as the years past; the church and Town Hall being completely black. The impact of the smoke cloud which permanently covered the Potteries was most noticeable when one travelled a few miles out of town, except at times when business was poor or during 'Wakes Week' when all the 'potbanks' were closed for the week's annual holiday... I was one of the fortunate few boys in a class of 45/50 whose families went to the seaside for a holiday, Rhyl, Colwyn Bay, some seventy miles away and it was when we were returning by train that the impact of entering the pall of smoke was dramatic. I used to think I could never get used to such pollution after the days of breathing clean fresh air at the seaside, but within days, back at school, normal living returned. Of course, all towns had high pollution from the coal fires but the Potteries, like all industrial areas had the added pollution from 'The Works'. But I think, on reflection that the London Smog I was to experience as a young man later was a much

BURSLEM OLD TOWN HALL – by day

BURSLEM OLD TOWN HALL – by night

more serious threat to health than the Potteries 'puther' (smoky atmosphere).

Walking twice a day to school, all meals at home, was routine but on occasions, during these periods, some incidents were imprinted in my mind. Looking back they were valuable periods when all sorts of topics were discussed with one's pals, the beginning of a social behaviour and understanding or otherwise of other peoples views. Sadly, the motorcar has generally eliminated those times, free from parental and teacher surveillance in which natural development could take place with one's own generation.

Hill Top School which I attended, the babies' class at the age of 4/5 and Primary until eleven was only at the top of Hall Street where we lived. Mothers escorted us to school during the early years but later, the habit was to call or be called for by boys in the nearby streets and as a group walk together discussing all sorts of subjects from bird nesting, football and any of our latest escapades, particularly when a brush with senior folk's authority had occurred. We also had to pass a Catholic School, set back halfway up Hall Street where a rivalry existed in all schoolboy pursuits, from sports, fisticuffs, you name it, these sometimes developed into major snowball fights when the winter provided the ammunition. I think we did seem to have many snowy winters probably because the Potteries were some distance from the sea, the nearest coast seventy miles away. The snowball fights sometimes got a little out of hand because groups of more than thirty boys would battle it out charging backwards and forwards and I remember on one occasion we continued into the classrooms, which I'm sure must have brought some reprimand from the teachers!

The front of St Joseph's Church

Father Browne is remembered by many Burslem people as a forceful and charismatic personality. Described as 'tough' and 'tenacious' he was nevertheless known for the abounding generosity that he showed to poor families of Burslem in the 1920s and '30s. Also, it was not unknown for him to eject drinking men from local pubs, with the words 'Go home to your wives!' and in the event of pub disturbances and fights the cry "Send for Father Browne" was often heard.[14]

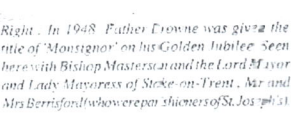

Right . In 1948 Father Browne was given the title of 'Monsignor' on his Golden Jubilee. Seen here with Bishop Masterson and the Lord Mayor and Lady Mayoress of Stoke-on-Trent, Mr and Mrs Berrisford (who were parishioners of St. Joseph's).

When Monsignor Browne died in 1956 his funeral was attended by a huge number of people and crowds lined the streets of Burslem and followed his funeral cortège to the cemetery some distance away.

Published by kind permission of A Davenport

34

8

There was always a certain animosity between schools in the neighbourhood and particularly in my case the Catholic School. On one occasion, when walking past the Catholic Presbytery with my pals, I was suddenly stopped in my tracks from behind, with Father Browne's walking stick hooked around my neck! I cannot remember his query but it was a practice of his to ask the caught 'lamb' if he was responsible for some misdemeanour carried out on one of his boys. Father Browne was a picturesque figure to us in his black habit and heavy shining boots, just visible underneath his skirt when walking with his crooked stick. He was a jovial man with a ruddy cherub like face, which my father suggested was enhanced by his daily 'tipple'. The Presbytery was normally a quiet place but I understood on occasions sounds of lusty singing emanated from the building indicating happy times when Father Browne was entertaining guests attended by the resident house-keeping Nuns, who also taught at the school.

His crowning glory was a large round black hat with a wide upturned brim which when one of us asked why it was so shaped, he replied, with a twinkling smile, "To catch the wonderful dew from Heaven, my boys". We sometimes could not understand his foreign accent which was of course an Irish brogue but he may also have had difficulty interpreting our broad 'Staffy Cher". The Presbytery where he lived was a large imposing house with double-bay windows in its walled, iron railed garden which stood out in sharp contrast to the small terraced houses in the street. It was adjacent to a small building which was demolished during my time at Hill Top School, and an impressive new church with a tall square tower built on the site.

When I became more adventuresome I used to go to school the 'back-way', along Murhall Street and round the back of Wades pottery negotiating an old marl-pit which was being filled with rubbish from the factory. My entry to the Sytch was made along a sandstone shelf, on which the factory was built and many times I would watch through the window, a 'Thrower' making eggcups on his rotating wooden disc. It was driven by his woman assistant rotating a large heavy hand-wheel which drove the potter's wheel by a rope belt. The small plug of clay was quickly transformed into an eggcup with his skilful wet hands and deftly separated from the table with a cheese-cutting wire and carefully removed to join others on the long carrying board. His 'lady' seemed to provide all the manual-labour, ensuring clay was kneaded to the right consistency, weighed to the correct amount and placed in batches alongside him. At the same time giving the four-foot hand wheel power to maintain its momentum during the 'throwing' period.

At other windows men were working machine driven metal bowls into which chalk moulds were placed. Then a measured wad of clay was thrown into the mould. A metal forming rod on an arm operated by the potter, was then lowered into the mould, excess clay pressed out thus forming the inner form of cup, basin etc. After a drying period, the item was removed from the mould, thus providing a uniform article in shape and thickness and much quicker than the old method. On reflection, I may have been witnessing the last of the original potters who had the skill to produce quality hand thrown ware. Also his hard-working lady assistant, most likely married, and after her stint at the 'Potbank' would have to provide meals etc for her family when she arrived home! A large percentage of married women worked in various ways at the pottery firms as well as taking a pride in keeping a clean and orderly home. In passing, most of the motive power for the factories was provided by horizontal steam engines with numerous rope drives carried between buildings and transferred to line shafting which in turn drove the relevant machinery.

As I grew older my adventure areas with my pals expanded further afield, with stern warnings from my Mother to behave myself and to know where we would be, with strict instruction to return at a prescribed time.

There were many places in the Potteries potentially dangerous for children, large holes, where red marl had been excavated from which to make tiles, teapots, earthenware pipes etc. Some were fenced off but most easily accessible to adventure seeking children and always prohibited by our parents. A number were near my home, one in particular had steep sides and filled with rainwater, many feet in depth and a no-go place for me.

Everyone was deeply shocked when a young boy was drowned in its dark waters. The same evening of the accident, my father took me to the pit and down to a precarious ridge a few feet above the water, which was used by playing children. He then asked me what I would do if I slipped in now? I immediately replied, "Oh, you would pull me out Dad" to which he said, "But suppose no one was here, which happened when that poor boy was drowned today and he couldn't swim?" I was left to ponder and made the obvious answer, "I should learn to swim". The impact of that evening will always be imprinted on my mind, the sober atmosphere with the knowledge of the boy's death some hours before and never daring to admit to my father that I had been there days previously. Needless to say I started to learn to swim and eventually obtained a life saving certificate. In later years I was to appreciate my father's sensible care and understanding, sometimes emphasized with a strap.

West Port Lake and nearby Bradwell Wood were popular holiday/weekend play venues. I don't know whether the lake was artificially created but was well over a mile round and a pleasant recreational area, rowing boats were available for hire and often used by my parents. It is nostalgic to remember the boatman calling boat numbers whose time was up, across the large expanse of water from the large wooden shed. We boys, unknown to our parents, used to, on hot summer days, bathe in our 'nothings', in small bays screened by rushes. Often having to stay in the water until passers-by had moved on, sometimes females would 'hang about' until we were shivering with cold delaying a clear run to our clothes guarded by one of our number who also acted as sentry. We had no towels but used our underwear to dry ourselves, dressing immediately! At least I never swam in the nearby 'Cut' (canal), often used by some boys, its dark yellow water laced with all sorts of refuse from the 'Potbanks', Steel Works, Stone Kilns etc., it being well used by horse-drawn narrow boats bringing coal, materials for production and collecting goods for export.

When I was some years older I was involved with what could have been a tragic incident on the lake. It was winter time, snow and hard frosts giving we boys much pleasure creating slides, which in some places were hastily spoilt by 'grownups' covering them with cinders and snowmen with many snowball fights. We always seemed to be at loggerheads with our elders which stimulated us to find play sites some distance from home. The West Port Lake was frozen solid for weeks providing a venue for safe skating with many people experiencing the unique pursuit of walking over the large expanse of ice; I seem to remember a brazier supported on a thick wooden platform on which chestnuts and toasted bread with cheese provided the participants with nourishment.

A thaw had begun and some small pools of water were in evidence in the centre of the lake although the ice was still thick near the edges. Against parental advice, I have no doubt my pals and other boys joined us playing football with a piece of wood. We were well aware of the danger and played away from the holes in the ice. However, one of my pals (I think Jimmy Blaize), running backwards to intercept the 'ball' fell into a pool. I think he could swim but the thin ice at the edges kept breaking when he tried to heave himself out. We instinctively went to help him but ominous loud cracking sounds made us hastily retreat. Fortunately, one of us ran over to some men shouting for help and one immediately ran over laying flat on the ice attempting to reach Jimmy but to no avail. Two of his companions anticipating the problem had obtained a ladder from the boat shed and carefully, laying it on the ice pushed it toward Jimmy, who was beginning to despair but we encouraged him to keep on treading water. On instruction from the men he managed to hold on to the ladder while they, with careful strength pulled him until his body moved onto thicker ice, when they were able to reach him. How long he had been in the ice cold water seemed an eternity to us but he was blue with cold and when the men knew we lived about two miles away told us to get him home as quickly as we could. So with us encouraging and helping, at first by supporting him between us, ran all the way home with frequent stops but making him 'run on the spot' whilst regaining our breath. By the time we reached home we were all hot and Jimmy literally steaming! As I recall he was none the worse for 'wear' after his ordeal. How lucky we were and grateful his parents to the men who were fortunately at hand and bravely carried out the rescue which, without doubt saved our pal's life!

Jack Goodwin, a friend of my father, was an accomplished skater often to be seen performing on the lake. In those days not many people could ice skate and Jack soon drew a crowd when performing intricate figures on the ice. He explained to my father and me that the true skill was to be able to repeat a figure on the ice over the marks of the previous one. I'm sure he influenced me to learn to skate and my father bought a pair of second-hand skates which were much too big projecting, 1½" beyond my toes! They were steel blades fitted to a steel frame which clamped onto the boots when tightened with a spanner at the heel. Consequently, although I managed to be able to skate a little with them, being very heavy and too large with damage to my boots my attempt to skate was limited and because hard winters were infrequent.

CHAPTER TWO

HILL TOP ELEMENTARY SCHOOL

MY ELEMENTARY BOYS SCHOOL

THE BABIES AND GIRLS SCHOOL DURING MY CHILDHOOD

When I moved up from the babies classes, which were part of the girls school I entered a more demanding time. The boys' school was on the same site but segregated with a Clinic and the Caretakers House in between the 'play-yards'.

As I remember there were two large rooms on the ground floor both with folding, sliding wooden partitions with windows in the upper half, thus forming four classrooms. Entry to them from the schoolyard was through a cloakroom, which had a number of iron frames with suitable hooks. A stairway from the cloakroom led up to one large room with a similar partitioning arrangement to the ground floor, forming two classrooms. The wooden floors from the front section were terraced to accommodate desks with hard wooden tops and tip-up seats supported on cast-iron frames.

The Headmaster's desk was in one of the lower rooms mounted on a small platform suitably placed so that he could observe activities through the glass partition of the adjacent class. Because entry to the end rooms was through doors in the partitions there was always a certain amount of interruption in the transit room so visits to the toilet or any other excuse to leave the room was strictly limited. All rooms had a table and a lectern from which the teacher conducted the lesson and was able to illustrate with text or sketches on a blackboard behind the table or one supported on an easel, behind which hung a bamboo cane! I clearly remember our headmaster and two other teachers, the others would need a schoolmate to recall and 'trigger off' my memory cells.

Mr Millington, the head master, (pictured with standard 111) was to make an example of me before class, for one of my misdemeanours, on instruction by my father so I need no prompting to remember him! It was due to me not returning home directly after school on some Fridays causing my Mother unnecessary worry. With other boys we would find many interests in the neighbourhood, arriving home very late, but always in time for tea. Persistent scolding from my Mother failed to have the desired effect and Father was told. I knew I was then in real trouble and suffered a weekend of mental anguish wondering when the leather strap (the strop for his 'Cut throat' razor), was to be un-hooked from its place on a cupboard beside Dad's chair.

Monday morning arrived and no punishment but as I was about to leave for school my Father handed me a letter with instruction to give it to my headmaster. He told me what was in it with the casual remark that he thought my companions might benefit witnessing whatever punishment Mr. Millington thought was necessary. It was a harrowing walk to school and also after I had handed the letter to my headmaster, knowing a 'sentence' awaited me. Eventually the moment arrived when I was called out to stand before the class whilst the letter was read to very attentive schoolmates. The gist of it was the worry parents suffered when children did not arrive home at an expected time and knowing that we were most likely causing mischief or a nuisance in out of bound places. I then had to hold, first the left hand followed by the right receiving 'two of the best' with a cane which whistled through the air when in action. The physical pain was borne with grit and with a vigorous rubbing and blowing in the smarting cupped hands. But the embarrassment of the letter reading will always be imprinted in my mind and I'm sure had a lasting effect, no more late homecomings. Whether my adventurous companions took note I cannot remember.

Caning during my time at Hill Top was used sparingly and contributed to reinforcing discipline, much needed with classes of 45/50 boisterous boys full of pent up energy, it was always expected to be suffered with a brave front and for some unknown reason (schoolboy folk-law), a few hairs across the hand were supposed to alleviate the pain and hairs from a 'copper knob' could break the cane! Breakages did occur but I suspect it was due to a weakness at the bamboo rings. Most probably assisted with a surreptitious penknife cut at the appropriate point by a previous sufferer. When it did happen the victim seemed to grow in stature as he returned to his desk, but the temporary triumph was mitigated by the teacher producing a replacement and showing his approval of its potential by swishing it before us making an ominous banshee sound, with the remark, "I wonder who will christen my new cane!" I suppose the canes were supplied by the Education Authority for the teachers to use to indicate or emphasize points on the blackboards, which they did, and found a double use for further emphasizing points not on the blackboard! Thinking back one wonders whether they were made especially for school use being thin with curved handle and would not provide much support as a walking stick. But I recall Charlie Chaplin used a similar cane most dexterously with many entertaining effects.

Strangely enough, years later when studying for my Second Class Certificate of Competency, Mr Tom Bennett, co-author with Peter Youngson of the book (Practical Mathematics for Marine Engineers), was lecturing on the case hardening and tempering of steels. He remarked, thereby claiming our undivided attention that the urine of a red headed boy was ideal for tempering steel. A 26 year old, young at heart, pupil in our class of eight, asked whether the urine from the female of the species would be better? Mr Bennett replied that it was an interesting point and suggested that Mr. ---------- should carry out a controlled experiment, the results of which may be worth publishing and added that the countries from which the specimens were taken, be recorded, so that the high technical standard expected from marine engineers be maintained!!

On the question of discipline, two of our Hill Top teachers served in the Great War, Mr Mason had been a pilot in the Royal Flying Corps, the compass in its gimbals from his plane was a permanent fixture on a shelf in his classroom, and the other, whose name I cannot remember, a Major in the Army but he is pictured with Standard V, 1927. It would have been taken, after what was a form of the Eleven Plus and I seem to remember that a small number of us were subject to extra attention with our studies before the examination and after passing went to Burslem Central Boy's School. More of that later. Perhaps my generation were fortunate in that we inherited a form of discipline (sadly disappeared) from teachers who had served in the Armed Forces and there must have been many schools with similar teachers.

There was no canteen in most Elementary schools I suppose there was no need because children lived within walking distance, indeed I believe there was only a limited facility in the teacher's room. An hour and a half was allowed for lunch break, which provided ample time to walk or cycle home for a nourishing 'Dinner', it being the main meal of the day which most parents took together. Regular walking or cycling to and from school helped to keep one fit plus the simple wholesome food cooked by our mothers. Obesity was rare and mostly inherited.

It is only when one tries to recall times in early life and what one did, physical, mental or by observation that memory proves clear, in some aspects doubtful and dormant in others until reminded by sight or by companions of that time. Some incidents are imprinted by trauma or personal pain but routine subject matter seem to fade forever. In my case school studies fall in the latter category at Hill Top but more clear when I later attended Burslem Central School for Boys.

At Hill Top, there were six classes and presumably six teachers which could have included the Headmaster but I can only remember two besides him. One teacher, in the main, taught all subjects to his class. First thing in the morning after register call, a short religious service took place when we chanted a few lines of religious text followed by the Lord's Prayer. Learning 'times tables' by heart proved invaluable throughout my life followed by mental arithmetic, reading and writing but spelling was one of my weak subjects. Physical exercise was conducted in the tarmacadam schoolyard also our leisure breaks (playtime) etc.

Competition among we boys was always present whether it be academic or physical and often emphasized with aggressive behaviour (part of the male characteristic). Most of our games required skill or strength, sometimes cheating, which invariably led to scuffles and fisticuffs, always stopped if seen by teachers. Sometimes differences were settled between individuals by arranging to fight after school hours outside school premises. When differences occurred, the more aggressive boy would challenge the other by beating him on the chest three times with a clenched fist accompanied with the verbal remark which sounded like, "Wun tow thray arm boss oerthay" (One two three I am Boss over you), loud enough for the surrounding boys to hear. If one disputed the challenge a time and place was arranged, outside and after school to fight. The news of the forthcoming fight would quickly spread, verbally or sometimes by note passed, from under one desk to another during lessons.

My quick temper and perhaps the need to retaliate to bullying paved the way for me being the participant in a number of fights. Indeed when I left to attend the Central School I remember the Headmaster commenting, "That I was always fighting" a statement which surprised me. On reflection, and looking at my school photographs there was quite a difference in the type of home from which we came. Therefore some jealousy existed, relieved by fighting, often resulting in bloody noses but no serious injury, very often your opponent became a good pal. It was a benefit in learning to live with boys from different backgrounds and to be more tolerant with the ones from poorer (financial) homes but often, richer, caring homes. My later sea-going years again provided a working/living together life which I'm sure taught me tolerance and understanding of men from different backgrounds and cultures, a valuable education.

With regard to my schoolboy fights, there were two venues where I 'performed', one was down the adjacent lane behind school, past the 'Ragged School' and in the precincts of a 'Potbank' and the other, a waste ground down the Back Sytch behind Wades factory. One encounter near the Ragged School I remember well. It was a hot sultry afternoon where a dozen or so excited boys formed a ring with the usual elaborate removal of jacket or 'Gansy' (Pullover) and handed to the 'Seconds'

The school picture, Standard 111, shows me, fourth from the right, below the boy on the back row who fainted.

Picture, Standard V. I'm on the same row, third from the right, with Jimmy Blaize (saved from the frozen lake), third from left, third row down.

by the contestants. A boxer's stance would be taken up with a feint or two but once a blow had been struck it became a melee of flying fists. My opponent was bigger than me but was one of the boys whose gansy was, most likely, the only covering he wore and did not take it off. My glasses, jacket and tie were in the safe custody of a pal and the open necked light shirt provided some ventilation from the heat of the battle. Clouds of dust rose from the scuffle when suddenly my opponent fainted and fell over backwards. Some minutes later he recovered and the now silent boys, including me, heaved a sigh of relief knowing that he was not seriously hurt. We shook hands and that was one of the shortest fights I had. His faint may have due to the heat and dust, but under-nourishment could also have been a factor. I was one of the lucky ones who had adequate food.

There were other fights in which I was privileged to take part. One at the site overlooked by Wades, when having fared the worst I was lying down to stop my nose bleeding, when one of the audience passed a derogatory remark about me, and my responding that I would take him on when the bleeding had stopped! Strangely enough, I have no clear memory of the outcome of my encounters, but most certainly have at arriving home with blood stained handkerchief, shirt etc., and seeing my Mother's anguish. She would quickly removed the affected garments and rinse them to help remove permanent staining. Later pleas by her to Father to complain to the headmaster were unsuccessful with his remark "He has to learn to stand on his own two feet". One thing I am certain, no real harm was sustained, all fights were fair, one to one no cowardly attack by more than one on an individual. Afterwards, in most cases, a quiet respect often resulted and sometimes the beginning of a friendship.

However, there were 'Tribal wars' between schools and neighbourhoods, from which I was restricted by my mother, when she knew. The snowball fights were good fun, until, on occasions, small stones were used to form the snowballs in order to increase their velocity, potentially dangerous practice. But the stone throwing battles were very dangerous. I have no idea what caused them to start, but think small differences between boys on some of the waste grounds, often being covered over with rubbish from the tile and pottery factories provided stones, clinker and broken earthenware, ammunition to hand with which to attack one another. News quickly spread for reinforcements from the opposing neighbourhoods (Dalehallers-Hilltopers) with sometimes twenty or thirty boys on each side. When I was able to get near the fringe of hostilities and saw the clouds of missiles flying through the air, I beat a hasty retreat! One time I remember seeing a large boy, possibly a backward teenager was skimming a section of broken plates, two to three feet above the ground. He was known for this ability and had one or two small boys supplying him with broken earthenware.

I remember some of the games we played in the schoolyard. One was 'Rallyango', there may have been other names and I assume it meant, 'Rally and Go'. Two teams would be agreed, four or five in number, and one team would 'form an elongated back', the first boy supported by a wall. Then the other team would leapfrog onto the waiting 'dragon back', victory being claimed if the dragon was able to support the other team without collapsing, then the procedure being reversed.

Collecting cigarette cards was a popular hobby, 'spon', (new cards) would be cherished, and swapped, in order to complete a set. The only game with them I remember was to stand a number against the wall, a line marked about a foot away, the Den, and (The Dorks), about eight feet from the wall, then your opponent would attempt to knock them down standing at the baseline by flicking or flirting, as we called it, his cards like a flying saucer, claiming any he knocked down, but sacrificing those which fell in the Den. Needless to say, the cards used were soon damaged but before a game was started a serious inspection was made and the tatty ones eliminated, later to be exchanged for ones of better quality.

Many types of games were played with Stonies or Marbles, mainly in the school playground with a smooth surface. The former were the cheaper, made from baked red clay and coloured with paint which soon wore off and broke in some games where they were knocked off a line a few inches from a wall, with a 'Glassy' or steel ball-bearing. The better quality marbles were made of glass with coloured streaks through, which one still sees today and another source of green glass balls, were obtained from lemonade bottles which used the trapped ball as a seal in the neck. The most popular game was to draw a chalk ring, into which contestants would place an agreed number of marbles and from a base line attempt to knock out, and claim by flirting one's 'tore' from thumb and forefinger along the ground, claiming any knocked out of the ring.

We suffered many bruises and cuts whilst playing in the schoolyard, but I remember one incident when I fell backwards hitting my head hard on the tarmacadam. I was taken home in what I can recall a 'Quiet World', most probably severely concussed. It was some days before the doctor allowed me to return to school. Some years previously whilst sleepwalking I fell down stairs and was dazed for a time and I have since wondered whether the two incidents advanced or retarded my mental condition!

CHAPTER THREE

HILL TOP SUNDAY SCHOOL

It was only recently that I appreciated a little of the history of Hill Top Wesleyan Methodist Chapel after reading and seeing pictures of its former grand structure and remaining façade in Carmel Dennison's book, BURSLEM – PEOPLE & BUILDINGS.

The Façade, all that remains of Hill Top Chapel
Side View

My attendance at the Sunday school began at an early age, 4/5 years old I think, at the same time I started my elementary education and continued till my teenage years.

The Chapel at the top of Hall Street was only a few minutes walk from home but I'm afraid, not taken with great enthusiasm because it meant, for we boys, dressing up in our Sunday best suits and thereby being fully restricted from any interesting pursuits! There were occasions, however, when a keen interest was made to attend on the prize giving Sunday's each year to receive, provided one's morning and afternoon attendances qualified, a book or Bible. I'm sure, in my case, it did seem to provide an incentive. Also, in recognition for attending 'The Band of Hope' one evening every week, they were given a small potted geranium which, with mother's help reminding me to water it, usually provided a colourful display for many months at home. I also signed 'The Pledge', not to drink alcohol but cannot remember at what age and in retrospect wondered how many of us kept the promise. I seem to remember a certificate being issued to the potential abstainers but cannot remember what happened to mine. I've no doubt if it was still available it would be of interest as a memento of those years but never to be exhibited because I disqualified myself many years ago.

The ground floor was used for the children's Sunday school, a spacious hall with a stage from which we were addressed and was an idea place for other forms of entertainment. When we were old enough, in the morning after the children session of religious instruction we joined the morning service in the chapel above but were allowed to leave before the Minister's sermon.

Rear View

Anniversary Sundays were the highlight of the Sunday school calendar, being a very special service when we boys in our best suits and the girls in pretty white dresses, were all accommodated on a tiered platform around the pulpit. Some of us were lucky enough to have a new suit for this occasion when the one uppermost criteria was who had the most pockets, the quality or cut of the cloth of no interest.

One particular anniversary will be remembered when myself and another boy were asked to 'man' the bellows to give the organ life because the electric blower had failed. I think it must have been the first time such a calamity had struck because when we were shown into the dark dusty, funny smelling secret compartment alongside the organist, the powers that be weren't sure how the hand operated gear worked. My mate and I could only just reach the large wooden handle and with our combined weight pull it down and assist upwards with our shoulders. A 'dummy run' showed that it was going to be difficult for us to supply the 'wind' needed when the organist was playing with both hands and feet bringing in crescendos of sound with the base pipes at full blast. Hastily a piece of string was attached to the 'works' and fed through a hole into our compartment with a six-inch nail on the end. Two lines

Were scratched on the bulkhead between which we had to keep the dangling nail, the higher one being our biggest worry because beyond that point the organ would begin to wail like a dying duck!

I shall never forget our frenetic activity in that dark stuffy hole. Jackets were soon off, ties and shirts followed and only when we knocked on the bulkhead during a heavy blast did the organists' assistant allow us to have the door ajar so we could survive. What wonderful relief we had when the Minister's sermon started, for the first time in our young lives we welcomed an event which previously we had never appreciated. But keeping that blinking nail below the minimum line was an horrendous experience for us especially towards the end of the service when we were very tired and sweaty but able to mutter Amen with relish and heartfelt thanks.

On reflection one wonders what the congregation's reaction would have been if they could have seen us behind the oak panelled door, the Organ Slaves. We must have looked like a miniature version of Galley Slaves, pumping away instead of many shackled men rowing a galleon. But in both cases with torsos gleaming with sweat in a confined gloomy atmosphere devoid of daylight. The galley slaves taking a well earned respite when a wind arose providing the energy, whereas for us a spell to regain our strength when the Preacher arose to stir the congregation with a 'storm' of words.

Encouragement to attend Sunday school was stimulated by giving book prizes when we obtained over a certain number of marks on our cards which were stamped for morning and afternoon attendances. Bibles together with a variety of books were presented at the end of term to the qualifying children and was a special occasion having to mount the platform to be congratulated by our teachers and the Minister or special guest, probably a sponsor. Some children were frequently successful but I think I was only presented on the odd occasion because outings with my parents when father obtained a combination motorcycle and sidecar, reduced my potential, but must admit the latter provided a greater appeal.

As a teenager, I was encouraged to teach a young children's Sunday school class but never felt competent even after attending a weekly evening instruction class. However, I was also attending three Night School sessions for my engineering Higher National Certificate, which gave me a bona fide excuse to leave religious teaching because the evenings clashed.

I'm indebted to Mrs. Milly Bloor, a dear friend, for her sketch (shown overleaf) which shows a perfect view of my old chapel and adjacent 'Potbanks' and my day school just out of sight around the corner on the right of the picture. My old schoolboy pal, Ewart shown in the pictures, Standard 111, 4th from left in the row below back row and 7th left, middle row Standard V, was her late husband.

HILL TOP METHODIST CHURCH

22

CHAPTER FOUR

BURSLEM CENTRAL SCHOOL

My school life changed considerably when I attended my new school, BURSLEM CENTRAL BOYS' SCHOOL, Moreland Road. It was a modern building compared with HILL TOP, with a girls' school on the same site and a much greater walking distance, twice each day because the midday meal was always at home. Walking to school was never a chore, out of bound adventures, homework, different views on many subjects, were discussed and I'm sure in retrospect, a valuable time away from the constant supervision of parents and teachers, learning to understand and cope with ones' contempories.

Six classrooms on each side of an assembly hall accommodated 30/4 boys in each; the communal hall was well ventilated with large skylights, which also provided illumination on the inboard side of the classrooms. Mr. J. Edwards, our Headmaster (Jimmy), had his desk on a plinth in the hall behind which was a cloakroom and at the other end a teacher's room. Outside toilets with a small covered area adjacent providing shelter when it rained in the play-yard.

The Assembly Hall, Burslem Central Boys' School.
Now a business company's office. The three classroom windows on each side have been blocked off making it much darker than when I was there. I can still visualise Mr Edwards's desk on the right-hand side of the red exit doors.

A separate two storey building in one corner provided the woodwork classroom above which was the Science Laboratory. Mr Harrison, our science teacher, I well remember, and in particular his opening remarks on our first lesson. "You are now in a dangerous place and must be attentive and very careful with how you handle all chemicals and containers". He then demonstrated the effect sulphuric acid had when a few spots from a pipette were dropped on to a piece of zinc. Immediately an obnoxious gas arose from the boiling area. He then demonstrated how the taste of a glass of drinking water was improved by adding a similar quantity of sulphuric acid. A vivid demonstration by sight and taste of the importance of dilution.

We had two woodwork teachers, I have mind pictures of them, the senior one again very strict, pointing out the danger with razor sharp tools and the importance of handling same with wood properly placed and secured before work commenced. He was also prone to demonstrate his displeasure when a work piece was spoilt by a rap with the item before putting an axe through it. I did have a small accident when working with a chisel, the wood tilted over and I sliced a small piece off my fingertip. First aid was rendered and I was taken a few hundred yards up the road to the Hayward Hospital where it was examined and surgically dressed, no further attention needed. The next day I discovered one of my classmates had 'rescued' my missing tip and was showing it in a matchbox to anyone interested. Obviously an entrepreneur in the making, because he was charging a halfpenny for a look at a bit of Swain's finger. Whether he gained chemical knowledge in the laboratory or skills in the workshop, his ability to make the 'quick buck' when the opportunity presented itself would stand him in good stead to make his way later on in life.

I remember with nostalgia some of the unusual characteristics of our teachers. Mr Budd, our French teacher, would on the occasion of one of us having difficulty with a French word or verb pronunciation would tuck the culprit's head between his legs and vigorously slap his backside. After my first year it was decided I would take the Industrial Course which meant French was omitted from my curriculum, my French form of punishment ceased. But no such luck with Mr. Kidd, our History teacher, his punishment was 'rendered' with the edge of a wooden ruler, the 'patient' suspended from the back of his pants, feet just clear of the floor, thus presenting a well moulded posterior to the wrist action strokes of Mr. Kidd's ruler. By gum – it stung, with a minimum amount of energy from our dedicated teacher.

He was also our swimming instructor, strict but caring. Our swimming lessons, which included training for Life-Saving Certificates, were taken in the Burslem Swimming Baths a few hundred yards down Moreland Road, the opposite side to the railway station. Heated chlorinated water was used and to ensure we were washed clean, Mr Kidd conducted a personal observation that we all showered thoroughly under the tap water shower and checked every boy before leaving the baths that their hair was fully dry by hand testing the hair at the nape, often forgotten, being out of sight, like the backs of our shoes after cleaning. The cold shower during the winter months was much resented but could never be missed by the vigilant Mr Kidd, his sensible precaution to mitigate the chance of catching a chill or cold.

Mr Beach, our Geography teacher, was always smartly dressed and had a mincing style of walking, he was also the sports teacher refereeing the football on The Triangle, an open piece of waste-ground between the park and railway line, no grass, just dirt, odd stones and projecting bits of saggar providing an additional element to our vigorous game of football.

On one afternoon Mr Beach decided he would like to play, so asked in the classroom the size of our football boots, it so turned out that I was the only boy with size nine, the size he required (I had a large foot three sizes bigger than the average boy of my age, thankfully it stopped growing at ten). We were all ready for action, so Mr Beach and I exchanged footwear, me feeling very superior in his highly polished brown shoes and couldn't resist, after he had left the room, giving a demonstration of his 'highfalutin' walk with hand on hip to the great appreciation of the class.

I seem to remember our English teachers' name was Mr. England and although having the same qualifications as the Headmaster, was much disliked by his pupils for his overbearing manner. He didn't seem to have the experience in teaching, he used the cane and on one memorable incident, one of our classmates, (he was as big as Mr England), was brought forward for punishment after a verbal degrading. A confrontation developed between the two and resulted in the role of teacher and pupil being reversed, Mr England escaping punishment by a mad exit from the classroom with us restraining our cane-waving classmate. Later he returned with Mr. Edwards, our Headmaster, the culprit was sent from the room and the class informed, by Mr Edwards, that intolerable behaviour would be severely dealt with, parents informed and with the possibility of being expelled.

During my last year Mr Edwards arranged for the school to present Gilbert and Sullivan's 'Mikado' at the New Town Hall, Burslem. Quite a spectacular event requiring many hours of rehearsal, costumes and 'props' borrowed from a theatrical agency and I remember very successful. Needless to say my ability to act or remember lines excluded me from the grand stage but gave me the opportunity to be one of the 'shining stars' to sell chocolates and ice-cream to the audience.

SPORTS DAY 1930-36

The picture in THE WAY WE WERE, March 1996 of Burslem cricket ground, Cobridge, brought vivid memories of our annual sports days which were held there.

I enjoyed running, indeed my Father took a keen interest in my running ability because during the years I attended Burslem Hill Top Junior School, after some persuasion on Saturday afternoons, he would get me to run against older boys giving some of them yards start in order to develop my capability. Perhaps it was his enthusiasm that made me reluctant to train because it became a chore. He was very disappointed later when I was a teenager and did not want to progress to more serious running. However, with hindsight, I'm sure my interesting life would have perhaps been mundane when one sees how present day sports people have to sacrifice so many pursuits in order to reach a high standard in their chosen sport. In any event, my joining the Merchant Marine some years later, would not have been conducive to any sports other then deck quoits, tennis or golf.

However, I'm sure his training contributed to my success in the Burslem Central Sports Days Events, which always claimed my full participation. There were many individual as well as team prizes and a gold medal for the champion boy. A wide range of events provided a chance for all boys to join in with different abilities: 100, 220, 440yd flat, 100, 220yd hurdles, high and long jump and hop, skip and jump, throwing the cricket ball, with team events for the four house colours.

Throughout the three years attendance, we boys in each form were divided into four house teams represented by colours.... Charts in the assembly hall displayed points gained by the teams for the different pursuits and skills carried out in the school. On a recent visit to Burslem I was able to take a picture of the assembly hall, now a part of a business complex, the room darker due to the absence of the classroom windows each side, but I could still visualise the headmasters desk at the end mounted on a platform. Looking back, what a good system the charts proved to be. They provided a form of self discipline whereby all boys were aware that their capabilities, good, poor or indifferent contributed to a competitive team effort made public, by the charts displayed to the whole school. Points were allocated so that the different characters of we boys be they studious or sporting, were taken into account.

Regarding sporting activities, first year boys were given an advantage since the older ones were given handicaps based on their performance on previous years. I think I was given 20-30 yards start in my first 440yd race and won comfortably and did well in other events. However, the next and final year my handicap was dramatically increased and all boys entering for the championship were scratch starters. A number of events were compulsory for the championship which I managed to win in my final year without winning an event, a number of seconds and thirds which, I think, demonstrated the effectiveness of the handicap system.

Any boy who had a flair for sports was encouraged and his advantage was reduced by his handicap, furthermore his energy was additionally expended because he would invariably be expected to enter the house events. All in all it was a demanding day for everyone, starting about ten in the morning with prize giving late afternoon. All boys had to take part, which necessitated many heats with semi-finals and meant that an enthusiast was running all day. On the day I won my medal I was sick about mid-day, most probably due to the excessive action after a hearty breakfast. This lesson I took note of later when I represented the school in the County A.A.A. sports, I think, on Port Vale or Stoke City's Football ground. We enjoyed the day but Burslem Central was unable to win any of the events or any member of our team selected to represent Staffordshire, judged on their performance. No doubt we failed on merit but it was noticeable that some schools had been given better training and provided with bona fide athletics gear. We only had our football rig to wear; I remember my shirt was too long so I had to tie a string around my waist to keep it away from my knees. Ordinary plimsolls were not the best to run on grass, whereas some of the high school lads had spiked running shoes, something we had never seen on our sports days. Also most of us were entered into more than one event and the lad who won the 440yds, I think from Hanley High, only ran in that race and I noticed a coach massaging his legs with oil in the dressing room before the event. Never the less we enjoyed our sports and although disappointed at not winning we did not begrudge our opponents their victories.

The recent death of Sir Stanley Matthews and the picture of his funeral passing his statue in Hanley reminded me of my footballing years at school. In the first year, I played in the forward line but when Fred Steel (Nobby), our captain suggested I would be more effective as centre half, it became my permanent position. I believe Nobby played Internationals for Stoke City and afterwards became Manager of Chesterfield United. We must have played against Sir Stanley's team as schoolboys and I seem to remember Nobby was able to make Stanley work a little harder to get through, Happy Days! I also recall Nobby being very emotionally affected if we lost a match, seeing him shed tears of disappointment in the cloakroom when discarding our football rig.

Stanley Matthews, left with Freddie (Nobby) Steele
January 1933

Another Hanley boy whom I recall, Wainwright, (doubtful spelling), represented the United Kingdom swimming in the Olympics, he was provided with a taxi to take him to work etc. because walking or cycling was not beneficial to 'tuning' his body muscles for swimming. I cannot remember how he fared but his forte was the overarm crawl, a form of speed swimming in its infancy.

On the same page of THE WAY WE WERE, the picture showing the slag bougie emptying white hot embers at Shelton Iron and Steel, reminded me of the event because at Burslem during dark nights the momentary illumination was spectacular. Often one would look at the clock, I think about 10.30 and comment 'The slag trucks on time'. As reported, during the winter months, one could read a newspaper outside in the dark; strangers were startled by the phenomenon wondering what was happening. Its effect must have been seen many miles away from the tip, especially when the cloud base acted as a reflector.

My Class Burslem Central Boys' School
I am second left – front row

EXAMINATION SUCCESS
Burslem Central Boys' School

At the recent examination held by the Union of Educational Institutions the under mentioned pupils of the Burslem Central Boys' School gained successes in the first year senior course:-

English (S.I. stage) --- First Class, G. Millington; second class, W. Alderley, L.J. Ward, F. Brereton, S. Lawton, S. Swain, H. Bethell, A.E. Gower.

Practical Mathematics (S.I. Part 1.) --- First Class, H. Bethell, L.J. Ward, A.F. James, S. Swain, E.P. Maguire, L. Morgan; second class, C. Docksey, K. Mee, A.E. Gower, W. Adderley, G. Millington, W.E. Sparrow, S. Lawton.

Experimental Mechanics and Physics (S.1. state) --- First Class, C. Docksey, A.E. Gower, A.F. James, K. Mee, H. Bethell; second class, E.P. Macguire, G. Millington, S. Swain, J.L. Ward.

Geometric Drawing (S.1. stage) --- First Class, S. Swain, K. Mee; second class G. Millington, A.E. Gower, E.P. Maguire, W. Adderley, H. Bethell, W.E. Sparrow

Above an extract from the Staffordshire Sentinel 1930.

	First	Second
Adderley		3
Bethell	2	2
Docksey	1	1
Gower	1	2
James	1	
Maguire	1	2
Mee	2	1
Millington	1	3
Sparrow		1
Swain	2	2

CHAPTER FIVE

EARLY ADVENTURES

I am sure the first real adventure I remember, albeit vaguely, was my first flight in an aeroplane. I was very young, perhaps five or six, when Father arranged for me a neighbour's boy, Frankie Taylor, to be given a flight in one of the two bi-planes owned by Allan Cobham. His so-called 'Flying Circus' visited towns all over Britain during the summer months, when the public could experience small flights for the payment of 15 shillings (75p), which was quite expensive in the 1920's. Suitable farmer's fields near the towns were used which provided sufficient flat ground to enable the planes to get airborne, make a short circuit and land, able to clear trees or high hedges in their flight path.

A field on high ground adjacent to Bradwell Wood was the venue for my exciting trip. Father had already made, I think, his first flight and thought it would be a wonderful experience for me. After some discussion with the flying team it was arranged for Frankie and me to be strapped together in the open cockpit with its padded leather surround. Whether young children were eligible for what was then considered a pursuit with an element of risk and against regulations I never knew but knowing my Father it probably was. We must have been small sharing one seat and I could just peep over the right-hand side and my pal the other side of the cockpit. I well remember the roar of the engine, the bumpy take-off, the noise of the wind and when the plane banked I was able to see the field with 'smokey' Burslem in the distance. Still glued to the side of the cockpit my cheek was given a hard blow when we landed resulting in Father having to help remove and comfort a crying child after what he had hoped would have been a joyous and excited return. Indeed it had been before the landing and I wonder whether that unique experience gave me the desire to fly whenever the opportunity arose and I could afford it.

I could hardly contain my excitement during the journey home, what a story I had to tell mother, but when she saw the bruise on my cheek and how it had been caused, she was most upset. Father was in real trouble when she knew her precious child had been exposed to such danger. "The children could easily have fallen out of the cockpit," she said. He was in the 'Doghouse' for days and I expect he was not complimented by Mrs Taylor either! However, the flight with Alan Cobham (later to be knighted) was an example of caring parents, generally the father's urge for adventure and the mother's dedication toward the protection of their offspring, both essential requirements in the rearing of children.

Many years later, in 1939 during one of my early sea-going voyages, on the s.s. Fresno Star at Tacoma or Seattle, I'm not sure which, in Washington D.C., I was allowed to take over the controls of a four seater monoplane during a joyride, much to the concern of two shipmates behind. It was during the State's Bi-Centenary celebrations of joining the Union (42nd State, 11th November 1889). There were also two other events during the day imprinted in my mind, a parachute jump by a young lady and a demonstration of a remotely radio controlled Tiger Moth. During both events the American skill of showmanship was ably illustrated. The commentator introduced the lady before take-off and eventually after the plane had gained

s.s. Fresno Star

sufficient height, directed the crowd to watch her leave the plane, a tiny white dot in the sky. Everyone saw her parachute open and could follow her gentle descent downwards. Suddenly he exclaimed 'Oh my God, her chute has broken away!' There was a loud groan from the hundreds of spectators and I turned away to avoid seeing the hurtling body hit the ground when, after what seemed like minutes, he shouted 'She's managed to open her emergency parachute'. There was a tremendous sigh of relief and loud applause from the crowds when she landed.

The other event was a build up to a radio controlled planes flight, when it was wheeled onto the field. Again the commentator led the spectators through engine, aileron and rudder control checks by the empty plane. It then commenced its take-off but veered off course and stopped. Apologies from the commentator that it would be replaced with a stand-by machine, when he asked for a volunteer to man its controls, just in case as demonstrated, remote control was still in its infancy. Sure enough, an American sailor volunteered and was cheered by the crowd as he was given some basic instruction on how to use the controls, each move watched by the attentive spectators. The take-off and initial circuits were talked through by the commentator when, as one expected, it flew accordingly to the radio commands. Then, perhaps with some expectation from the crowd, the control packed up. What followed was some breath-taking flying by the Matelot from urgent instruction from the loud speakers.

What followed was the most erratic flying I have ever seen, the plane disappearing from view on a crash course and then from frantic instructions appearing in vertical climbs. Finally, after miraculously missing trees and surrounding buildings and many attempts made a very exciting, amateurish landing.

Earlier Tex Rawling's Flying Circus had given a wonderful demonstration of unorthodox flying, one of which was flying upside down only feet above the ground, the spectators able to read his name on the fuselage in the inverted position. Obviously, the Matelot was a member of the Tex Rawlings acrobatic team, but the entertainment value from the events was first rate.

31

Many years later, 1968-9, I attended a week's gliding course at Lasham, Hampshire and continued to be given instruction with our daughter Elaine (aged 15) at weekends but had to give it up as it was inconvenient for the family. Travelling from Surrey when the weather was suitable, and then only getting one a few minutes flight during a Sunday visit, was too time consuming. Even if I had gained an A certificate, constant practice was needed, with stipulated flying time, to retain one's certificate.

Chantal, Elaine's French Friend (on an exchange visit)

On my Gliding Course
SWS - Red Beret, Instructor - (specs), Pupil – Farmer's Wife

Awaiting take off – Elaine supporting starboard wing

Gliding is a wonderful sport/pastime, similar to sailing where one harnesses the element to travel, hopefully in the direction one wishes. Sailing and gliding are pursuits in which we humans try to imitate the sea and land birds, often quite amateurishly. My 5 hours 93 minutes flying time consisted of fifty take-off and landings, but took many, many days and long journeys to accomplish. During that time, in addition to the routine circuit training I was taught to cope with, cable break (the glider was towed with a 'pickup' vehicle), incipient spins, stalls and to soar in thermals. The long waits between flights were a boring feature for the family which emphasized the need for anyone to be able to enjoy it to the full ideally should own or part own a glider stored in a flying field near their home and also have freedom to fly whenever weather conditions are favourable. My period of instruction will be a treasured memory, an association with instructors and students, both men and women. Somewhere in the vast archives of the B.B.C. TV programmes is a brief recording of a 'take-off' with me under instruction, providing a back cloth, as we climbed in the sky, for the captions at the end of one of Cliff Michelmore's Adventure Holidays. Derek Piggot was the Chief Instructor during my time, who gave a flight to H.R.H. The Duke of Edinburgh in a T42b Eagle. Most of my flights were in a Slingsby T49 Capstan with an occasional flight in a K13 and my instructor suggested I needed to hurry with my training because daughter Elaine was at the stage to go solo but was underage until her 16th birthday.

As the sun was setting at the end of one day's gliding, Elaine and I had been fully occupied manhandling the gliders and in the queue waiting for a flight only seeing Grace when returning to the club-house for refreshments. The Polish instructor enquired if anyone would like to accompany him on the hangar flight, to which Elaine responded with speed, it being a free flight. She was in the process of strapping herself in the cockpit when Grace turned up in an exasperated mood, understandably, having spent many boring hours on her own. She enquired with 'some heat' "When are we going home?" and to Elaine "What was she doing in that glider?" The instructor obviously intending to pour oil on rough water, suggested that the best thing was for Grace to join us. To Elaine's disappointment and my surprise Grace took up his offer, was strapped in and I'm sure before she fully realised was three hundred feet airborne on her way to the hangar. Her anger was obviously overcoming her fear of claustrophobia and anything to do with gliding.

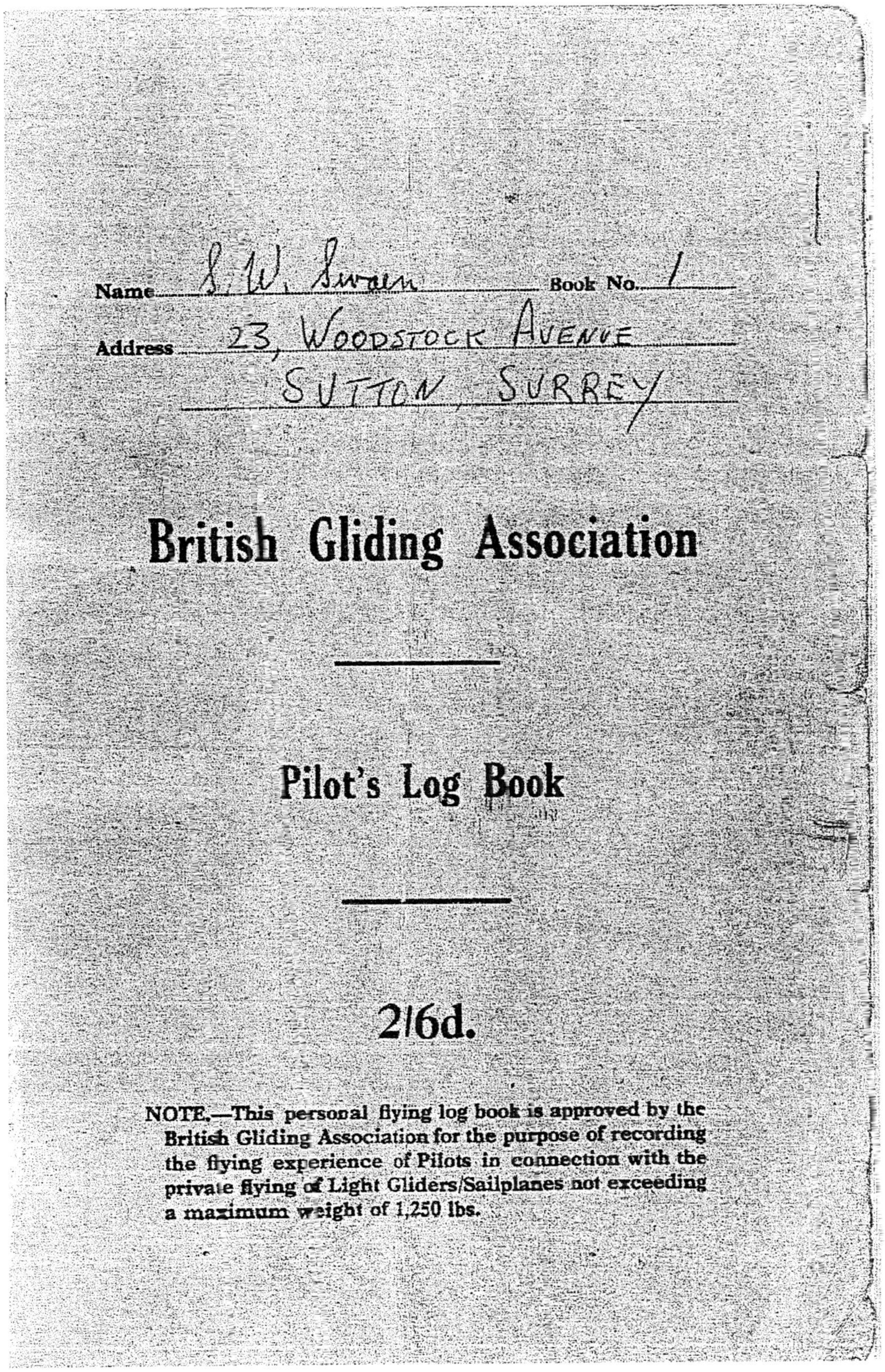

Name S. W. Swain   Book No. 1

Address 23, WOODSTOCK AVENUE

SUTTON, SURREY

British Gliding Association

Pilot's Log Book

2/6d.

NOTE.—This personal flying log book is approved by the British Gliding Association for the purpose of recording the flying experience of Pilots in connection with the private flying of Light Gliders/Sailplanes not exceeding a maximum weight of 1,250 lbs.

Year _____

Total Gliding brought forward 2.87? 5?

Serial No. of Flight	Date	Glider Type	Place of Launch	Type of Launch	Crew Capacity	Time in Air H	M	Remarks
1-6	17/6/68	T49	Lasham	W	P₂		29	Three experience, effect of controls, turns, assisted to ε landing. Cable break
7-9	18	T49	"	"	P₂		16	Further practice - 3 & 1 aerotows - Stalls ε incip. spin demonstrated. Cable break.
10-14	19	T49	"	"	P₂		44	Intro to soaring. Flying much improved. Assisted to ε take down landings
15-16	19	T21		"	P₂		10	Two good circuits, ε tidied down landings
17-21	20	T49		"	P₂		57	A good weather course with excellent progress. Has been instructed in
22-28	21/6/68	T49		"	P₂		54	all the basics of gliding ε is able to fly circuits unassisted
27-31	29/6/68	T49		"	P₂		13	Gliding took off ε landing with brakes. Needs practice now
								Extensive instruction & experience in circuit planning
32	13/7/68	T49		A	P₂	2	6	Stalls, spins - unusual circuit approach & landing - steadily flying
	3/8/68	K13		M	P₂	1	2	Take off, climb, explaining wind gradient, approach + first landings since
	9/8/68	T49	"	A	P₂	1	3	
		T49	"	A	P₂		15	Flying generally o.k. but needed speed / attitude
31-38	9/8/68	T49	"	M				control. Approach & descent at applicable speeds
	4/69	T49	"					various. Invite attention.

| | | | Time carried forward | | | 4 | 48 |
| | | | **Total time carried forward** | | | 4 | 48 |

Total time Single Seaters _____ No. of flights _____
Total time P.1 Multi-Seaters _____ No. of flights _____
Total time P.2 Multi-Seaters 4 - 48 No. of flights 3? 9

However, I return to my early adventures.

Many of my free times, always in the accompaniment of pals or younger brothers with Rip (the family terrier), were spent exploring the Westport Lake and Bradwell Wood areas some distance from home. Before I was lucky enough to own a second-hand bicycle, walking was the norm and should have always followed parental directed route i.e. through Dale Hall streets to Trubshaw Cross, down over the canal past a dusty firm which supplied materials for pottery manufacture, one of which was calcifying 'Ducker' stones which I seem to remember were delivered alongside, from narrow horse drawn canal barges. Continuing past the Gas Works with its huge gasometers and finally under the single line railway bridge to the small landing stage and boathouse which provided boats for hire on Westport Lake.

The more exciting and shorter route however, was across the fields behind St. Paul's Church past a huge marl pit supplying material for brick and tile manufacture, which later, when abandoned, filled with water, a dangerous place we used to play around and claimed the life of a small boy, a sad event, (Chapter one, page 10). Continuing past some garden allotments, well patronised by Mother for fresh vegetables and then over a fence onto the railway line which connected Chatterly Whitfield Colliery to Longport on the main Stoke to Crewe line. Being in a forbidden place always seem to heighten a sense of adventure. The infrequency of a tank-engine, either pulling a large number of empty wagons up a gradient back to the mine or with intermittent squealing of brakes taking a few loaded with black shining coal to the marshalling yard was seldom encountered. But we had plenty of sound warning to leave our game of seeing who could walk the furthest on the railway lines without falling off, to hastily move well away to watch 'Puffing Billy' pass, always with shouts from the driver or fireman not to trespass on a dangerous place with threats of the railway police being told of our whereabouts. Any such encounter hastened our use of the short cut. A similar dare was to see how far we could walk along the tops of old wooden sleepers used for fencing and retaining the embankment. On one side a drop of a few feet but on the other eight to ten feet of the unevenly spaced ends of the sleepers, some rotten, would break away, requiring a balancing agility and an ability to jump off the low side when one's equilibrium failed.

Westport Lake, in the main, was a staging post for our walks to Bradwell Woods but did provide many happy hours boating with our parents, in the summer, usually on Sunday afternoon. The shoreline was shallow with bays of reed beds except at the small landing stage by the boathouse, but reputed to be very deep in the centre. Therefore parental instructions were to play in the woods, to remove their fears of our drowning. Recently I asked Arthur Holt, whose parents were friends of my parents, how the lake originated. He thought it was first used as a football ground by Port Vale but was flooded when the canal, which is retained some feet above the area, burst it's banks. I recall hearing a similar story, when I was a young boy.

To get to the wood it was necessary to cross the main L.M.S. railway line by a footbridge near a chemical works at the North West corner, but a short cut was available using a farm crossing which I suppose was not for public use. Naturally we used it, running over quickly when the signals indicated no trains were due. Near the crossing gate on the lake side was a large pool of, what I think, must have been bitumen or pitch, probably dumped there due to some mishap with a railway wagon.

Ever looking for a dare it's soft surface, which varied considerably with the day's temperature, encouraged us to walk over small sections. When it was very soft we would run quickly so that our feet lightly touched the surface, speed being essential, and at places where only a few steps were necessary to cross over, competing to run across longer routes sometimes ended when someone failed to keep sufficient momentum and had to be pulled out with tar covered boots and stockings. I never got caught, but that was because I was not brave enough to take the risk. Goodness knows what punishment the odd victim suffered, I have no idea how the tar and grass, which had been used in a vain attempt to remove on site, was removed, since the sticky mess would transfer to clothing above the stockings as well.

The woods provided many interests, the most popular being climbing trees with associated dares, but in my visits never resulting in any serious damage other than splinters or scratches to bodies. Much more serious on arriving home was the damage to our clothes and the scolding which followed. During spring masses of bluebells were collected and carried home in large bunches for mothers, requiring jam-jars to contain them. One could never imagine that they, with many other wild flowers, would become protected species.

SWS   CHILDHOOD MEMORY
31-12-92.   OF
        HARECASTLE TUNNELS.

A very traumatic day will always be imprinted on my mind when a pal, who lived near me, severely damaged his knee. We would, I think, be about ten years old and the accident happened when we had ventured to see the Harecastle Tunnel, where canal barges travelled over a mile and a half underground in a dank narrow tunnel. There were two tunnels, the original running adjacent to the operative one, which used electrically driven tugs, powered with accumulators recharged between trips. We knew that the horse drawn narrow boats were 'footed or legged' through the old tunnel by the Bargee's, lying on their backs using the roof as a 'tow-path'. It must have been a real feat of stamina and endurance pushing a loaded boat with twenty five to thirty tons of cargo, depending upon the type of barge, through a dark, poorly ventilated wet slimy tunnel and in some places constantly dripping water. One can understand that, after the original effort to get the barge underway, the power needed to keep it moving is much reduced.

Many years later, in the seventy's, I purchased WATERWAYS HERITAGE by Peter Smith, January 1972, from the National Maritime Museum, Greenwich. It was interesting to learn that the Harecastle was the first main line tunnel; built by James Brindley (1766-1777) 2897 yards (1.65 miles) long, 5' 10" wide, 8' 6" high at water level. Also that two men, sometimes women, lying on their backs at the fore end pushing against the sides of the tunnel taking three hours to complete the task. On empty boats, one man could leg it through, lying on the cabin roof. It must have required the real skill by the helmsman/woman, most probably the bargee's wife, to ensure the boat kept clear of the sides with only candle or oil lamp illumination. Any deviation from a true course would allow the barge to hit the sides, thereby increasing the manpower needed or reducing the 'power men's' leg room. Most probably the penalty in that event would be that the helmsman/women would have to change places with a 'footer' who would have little breath for blasphemy. One imagines however, that changing places would be difficult and dangerous under such conditions but must have been necessary for the three-hour voyage.

One wonders what reaction there would be if a present day lorry driver and his mate were expected, on occasions due to engine failure, to push their lorries through a well ventilated, illuminated level tunnel over one and a half miles long and in a normal walking stance, not on their sides or backs in a dark dank cave.

The old tunnel could hardly be seen due to overgrown vegetation and I think it must have been a Saturday afternoon when we were there because, much to our disappointment, no movement of barges and the tugs were moored alongside the charging station.

On our way to Harecastle, we had played with a small derelict crane on the towpath which had most probably been used to unload materials for the steel works on the opposite side of the canal. Only the jib and a steel box, which would have housed the winding drum, remained and were mounted on a base, which had two projecting railway lines. We had given one another rides by pushing it around with one sat crouched between the tie-rods at the top of the jib and having the thrill of travelling over the canal some feet above the water.

Our interest was short-lived at the tunnel, so we commenced the journey homeward, stopping to have one last fling on the rusty old crane. Suddenly, during a ride, it stopped with a terrible scream from our pal. He had been pulling the box around when his leg hooked over a projecting railway line and was crushed underneath the box. We were all shocked by the accident and I have no clear memory of that traumatic time, except seeing that terrible wound and my panic as I ran along the towpath over the bridge and into the steel works for help. It was dark when I left the works but cannot remember how we got home. It must have been a terrible shock to his parents and I believe the damaged knee gave trouble for years afterwards. In retrospect, when I recall that terrible afternoon and with the knowledge of engineering related accidents, his body taking much of the force of the crane's momentum probably saved complete severance of my friend's leg.

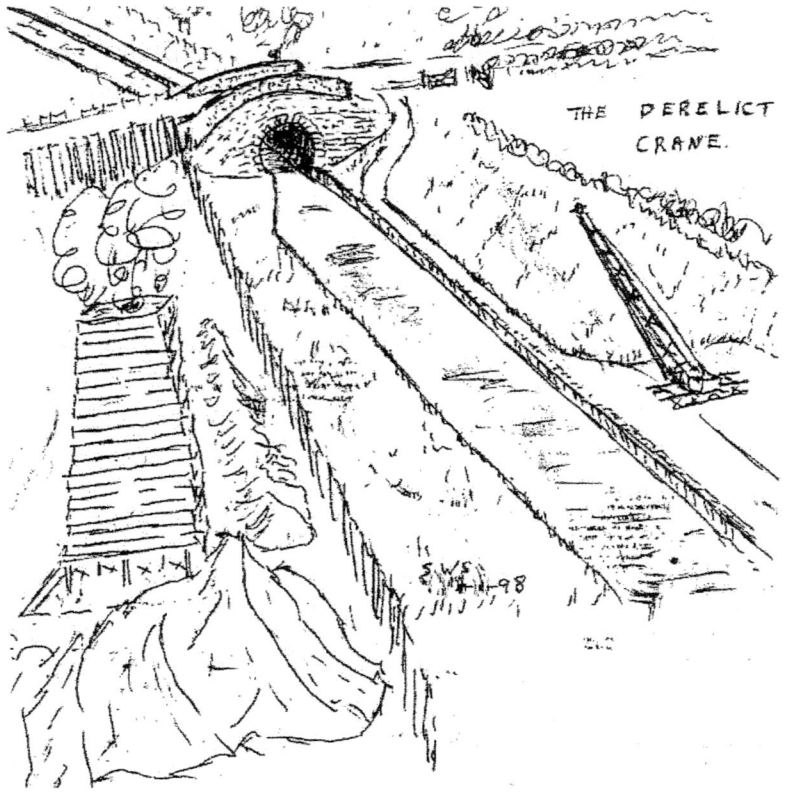

THE DERELICT CRANE.

Thank goodness the tapestry of life provides happy and humorous events, which help us to bear the sad ones.

I was asked one day by my father to cycle to Congleton, about ten miles away, on market day as he intended to buy a few Rhode Island Red pullets which he was going to rear for the kitchen table. He preceded me by bus and I was to act as 'Carter Pattison' bringing his purchase home on the back of my bike. It was a beautiful hot sunny day pedalling up and coasting down the hills enjoying every minute of my outward journey. When I arrived at the market, I found he had twelve young cockerels ensconced in a basket with their legs tied together covered loosely with a piece of burlap to prevent escape.

Even to me I thought the birds should have had more room, a thought that continued to worry me on the homeward journey especially as dad instructed me not to hang about, sensing he also wasn't too happy about the package on my back-carrier. Cycling with some urgency and apprehension under a hot sun heightened my thoughts for my live cargo especially as I used my Sturmy Archer low gear to climb hills I would have normally walked. Continuous glances behind assured me all was well until I reached the final very long steep hill approaching Tunstall, Kidsgrove Bank, nearly home. I was pushing my bike up the last quarter mile from the top when a passing lady drew my attention, with an angry look on her face, to my basket where a number of my cargo's heads were literally dangling over the edge, looking very red in the face, like me!

I hurried further up the hill when I 'spotted' a small pond in a field to which I thankfully pushed my bike and with some difficulty removed my hot birds, with some squawking, on their sides. Having previously watched fowl drink, I individually dipped each bird's head in the water holding it skywards for a few seconds and repeating the process. Whether they drank any of the water I shall never know but another lady from a house nearby had seen the spectacle of a young lad carrying out some unusual ritual with a lively bunch of one legged cockerels, and came over for a closer look.

Thankfully the airing had somewhat revived them and the lady advised me to get them home as quickly as possible, but she never bothered to offer me any sympathy. I pushed to the limit, thirsty, and mentally worried to death at father's displeasure if on his arrival home he found his birds eyes permanently closed before reaching the kitchen table suitably fattened. The remainder of my journey through Tunstall was mainly downhill, suffice to say those Rhode Islanders were well ventilated from my top speed dash home and they never 'looked back' after their feather raising pillion ride. They grew from strength to strength in our back yard with spells of free ranging outside on the wasteland behind our house. All were given names and father would point out the distinguishing features whilst he crushed small bones (left-overs) with a hammer, which he fed to them to build them up and improve the taste for the dining room table. Knowing him I'm sure he would use only rabbit, sheep or beef bones, never the frames of their brothers and I wonder whether all those years ago it built up my immunity to Mad Cow disease. Progressively during the year John, then Albert and so on, would be selected for the quick thrust of dad's penknife behind the wattle while being held firmly between his legs at the bottom of the yard over the grid. It was the two finest specimens who survived for Christmas dinner.

On a previous occasion father arrived home with a duck under each arm, probably form a similar market and I presumed they must have travelled 'first class' with him on the bus. Anyway, I was given the task to remove a number of 'Staffordshire blues' (water resistant bricks) from the bottom of the yard and construct a clay-lined pond for them. They also were part of Christmas fare and I'm sure we enjoyed the feast but perhaps also more pleased that the absence of their 'trade mark' in the yard would remove the skill needed for a safe passage to the toilet and back gate.

We always had a dog, all fox terriers and all called 'Rip', plus a cat and these provided company for the family, the dog on our safaris. Both had the use of the back kitchen and the dining room in the winter months. But none slept indoors at night, the cat usually eager to go, but the dog had to be ordered out, disregarding his wistful look to be allowed to stay. When I was old enough it was my responsibility to keep his kennel clean, during the cold months to ensure he had a warm straw bed, which the cat used to share at times. Father was obviously fond of animals, not all for the table, but when he arrived home one Saturday evening with a very young rabbit nestling in the vee of his overcoat we wondered, but he was a birthday present for one of my brothers. In those days wild rabbits were plentiful always to be seen hanging in the butchers shops and stalls in the markets, providing a nourishing and cheap meal. I often wondered why the women requested or were shown their innards before purchase and skinned. I'm told here in Norfolk it was to avoid buying a milky doe and the colour of the liver was important showing that it was healthy and nutritious. Robert, he was christened, most probably bought from the balcony in Hanley market where livestock was sold, and was provided with a hutch, which I made out of an old box and was located in the shed. Initially, he was kept ensconced, but he was allowed to be brought inside the house on occasions to be made a fuss of. However, under father's direction he was progressively allowed to roam in the back yard always with his hutch door open. Eventually, Robert became a free ranging rabbit, joining the dog and cat being 'shown the door' at bedtime. He became quite an attraction with the neighbours seeing him roaming outside, many times being chased by dogs but Robert always survived, often using a neighbours hen coup as a staging post, when he knew he couldn't make it home in one zig zag burst.

I think he had been part of the family for a year, quite a sight, cat, dog and rabbit sharing a place near the fire. I'm not sure whether father trained Robert to answer the call to receive a tit-bit as the cat and dog did and return to their respective places. A day to remember dawned when he went missing and we learned from a bed-ridden lady who used to enjoy watching his antics from her bedroom window, and saw a miner pick him up and pocket him early one morning. It was a sad event, many people asking where he was because he was quite tame enjoying tit-bits from the locals', which proved his undoing. We only hoped the thief put him to the pot because keeping him in a hutch after his natural freedom would have been traumatic.

My previous reference to immunity made me wonder whether modern day ultra cleanliness fails to provide antibodies, which may have been on offer to my generation by the living conditions in our homes when we were children. Often hearing the expression, "You will eat a peck (two gallons) of dirt before you die". Cleanliness was a daily chore, the red-quarried floor scrubbed with soft soap every day but the own made rag rugs only beaten outside against the yard wall. They acquired plenty of dust, the coal and ash from the kitchen fire and the dog, cat and rabbit used it for a nap, often all together, on every opportunity when no human was present. There must have been all sorts of life in the jungle of rag lengths.

Our rugs used to last a long time before being replaced but whether the availability of old clothes governed the transformation I don't know but I do remember how sweet the new one smelt. It was quite an on-going job for mother, I used to help cut up dad's suits etc. and when older, contributed in the making, pulling the pieces of cloth through the hessian base with a hooked tool which automatically released it to be knotted. With my artistic flair, marked out a colour pattern, with some misgivings from mother, for her out of date 'glad rags' to brighten up the overall funeral look.

Brother Austin was prone to accidents, often self-inflicted. One I remember well was when returning from one of our forays from the Westport Lake area, we had been looking longingly, no money in our pockets, in a sweet shop window in Ellgreave Street. The shop was part of the terraced dwelling houses where the front room had been changed to a shop, the small garden enclosed with iron railings, the tops of which formed a 'Prince of Wales Feathers' design. Vallance the youngest brother and myself with Rip left the shop through the gateway, but Austin decided to climb over the railings, standing on the top and jumped down. I had started to walk up the street when a loud clap and cry of pain made me look back to see Austin dangling with one foot trapped under the railing top. Luckily, his hands had hit the pavement taking the full force of his fall with his head just clear of the pavement. We managed to free his trapped foot and he escaped with a broken ankle. He was in terrible pain and my only thought was to get him home as quickly as possible, which I did by piggyback. I could feel the broken bones grating together with terrible cries of anguish from Austin. We were only about half a mile from home but in my ignorance transporting him as I did was the worst possible thing to do. However, I do not remember the ambulance or doctor's visit after we arrived home but his fracture healed and he had no trouble with the ankle afterwards.

CHAPTER SIX

MOTORCYCLING

It caused quite a stir in the family when dad told Mother that the few egg-laying hens we kept in a shed in the back yard had served their purpose. Mother wasn't too pleased especially when he intimated that he was interested in buying a motorcycle with sidecar and knowing that the real reason why her hens were for the table was to provide a garage for the motorcycle. I seem to remember that Mother thought fresh eggs for the family were more important to what she considered was a dangerous machine and pointed out that we had been well catered for, our pleasure trips and holidays by 'charabang' and train.

Father, like most males of the species, was interested in things mechanical. One of his hobbies was repairing watches when he spent many evenings with his spyglass over a white sheet of paper fiddling with tiny items with dire warning to the rest of the family to give him and the table a 'wide berth'.

Eventually, the BSA motorcycle and sidecar arrived after the brick wall at the bottom of the yard was demolished and replaced with a second gate. Even then it was a close fit and not easy to manoeuvre into the shed, which had also been modified.

In the 1920's public transport, either by train or bus, was most reliable and I imagine used by a large percentage of the population, also local electric trams (single deckers and noisy) provided an efficient frequent service between Tunstall and Longton, passing through Burslem, Stoke and Fenton.

I can recollect only one motorcar owner in our neighbourhood and he was a director of a small engineering firm and lived opposite in a bay-windowed house larger than the majority of terraced houses. Very few houses, as I recall, had a garage near the house. The odd ones where horses were stabled became useful so we had an advantage, able to house our own private, novel, transport machine at home. It also enabled Father, I'm sure, to enjoy many hours discovering its intricacies and at times getting it to start. On occasional Sundays when Mother's picnic spread was intended to be enjoyed in a country spot, it was consumed at home with Dad's portions in the back yard supplying him with energy to battle with hammer and spanners to establish 'life' again in our family carriage.

The pictures show a similar machine which I'm sure is the same model, but to me it was a large contraption, the green sidecar able to provide Mother in a sitting up position and me on a stool between her legs. There was plenty of room for my feet and the odd sanitary appliance stowed in the nose, with a folding down hood to protect us from the wind and rain when needed, and a celluloid windscreen, which wrapped around the front and clipped in position behind the small entrance door. A tubular frame carried the sidecar connected to the motorcycle and extended to provide a rack for cases and the inevitable picnic basket. The picture shows the motorbike with its long curving handlebars, which enclosed Father with brake, clutch, ignition and throttle controls. The long rectangular petrol tank, the front section with pump and sight glass showing the drops of lubricating oil gravitating to the engine, which Father adjusted accordingly, I suppose by his knowledge of his mechanical horses' need, chugging away between his legs. A gear change lever was mounted on the green tank with a white panel carrying the gold lined letters B.S.A. and companies badge (later to be called Bessie). A vee-belt drive between engine and rear wheel was later to become my job to retrieve from the road behind us when it broke with the palavar of lifting the rear end of the bike onto its stand, tool box out and another belt fastener fitted.

Acetylene lamps provided illumination, well ventilated to dissipate the hot gasses from the incandescent flame. A large one with an acetylene generator at the front with its water reservoir, drip controlled, over a carbide container and a smaller lamp on the sidecar. A small tail light clearly shown above the number plate became my responsibility to ensure it had not been jolted out or covered by the tails of my coat when I was promoted to ride behind Father, brother Austin taking my cosy stool and the last edition, Vallance, nestling in Mother's lap. Holding tight, sitting behind Father, gave a grand view of the countryside with some protection, but on the occasions when the British weather decided to wash away the cobwebs, wind assisted, it was my introduction to a man's world before the age of ten and at night extending my hand hoping against hope I would see the reflected red glow of the tail lamp. If negative, our three wheeled chariot was stopped and me being the chief assistant would dismount to relight with matches the tiny burner against the fury of the surrounding elements, something I was to experience in later years at sea, but in a one wheel mit propeller 'Sea Chariot' weathering the storms with no protection whatsoever but an exhilarating experience all the same. An interesting thought on the importance of our little red light, because the amount of traffic on the roads then was very sparse, also infrequent night driving (our vehicle was only licenced during the summer months). However, it was important for the red light to be seen because headlight beams at that time were short.

1914 BSA MODEL 'K' 557cc with BSA MODEL NO. 2 SIDECAR

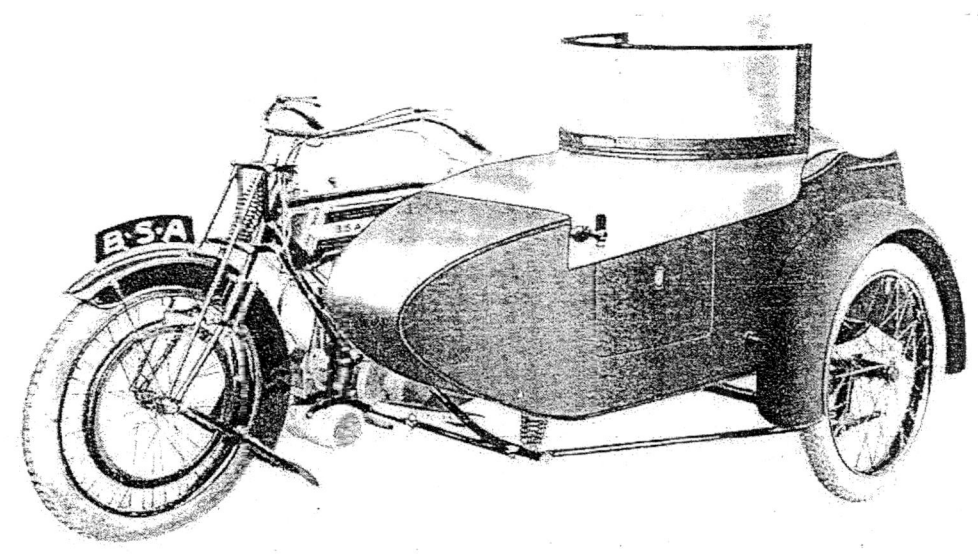

Pictures produced with the kind help from:
Cynthia Forster and Dick Lewis

The 1914 model 'K' 557 c.c. combination with B.S.A. model 2 sidecar picture does not have a rear seat and leg guards for the driver also the sidecar windscreen and hood, not shown. I note that spring suspension was only provided on the front wheel, the driver's seat and would have been on my pillion seat, but Mother's one wheeled chair having the luxury of being suspended on two coil springs. I can now appreciate with the rough roads of that time why it was exhilarating and no danger of anyone falling asleep when under way.

I certainly remember it's maiden voyage because I was the first passenger. Mother had persistently refused, point blank, to even try the sidecar for size, so, at the tender age of five or six, we set off. I must have been excited but only remember that at first whilst dad was looking down to change gear our course became a little erratic. Within a short time his cap blew off and was replaced with the beck (peak) at the back, which I thought gave his crouching figure a speedy look. Perhaps he was one of the pioneers because it became a customary sight. I don't remember if helmets were worn but goggles and flying helmets became a common sight giving the illusion of greater speed.

Our short journey through Dalehill, Longport and the testing climb up Porthil was accomplished, Father becoming more confident but passing over the common we suddenly came to an abrupt stop with a noisy metallic clang. We both must have been looking somewhere but not ahead because after I had pulled myself out of the nose of the sidecar (no seat belts in those days) and Father had regained his seat, having executed a hand stand over the handlebars. We found a gas lamp pillar on the outside edge of the pavement was firmly wedged between bike and sidecar with a tinkling sound of glass above. Our speed must have been low because after pulling the bike clear and off the pavement we departed homewards. It was probably early Sunday morning and we had the common to ourselves but I was given strict instructions not to tell anyone, especially Mother, where and how we had reached our turning point

There must have been many family outings on the old bike, but all trips were carried out with a sense of adventure and achievement arriving back home, sometimes much later than planned due to a puncture or mechanical problems, often stopping to assist with tools or knowledge with fellow travellers. Indeed it was custom and practice to hail any motorist stopped by the roadside to see if they wanted help. I guess we must have had the pleasure of travelling many, many miles during the six or seven years since my first ride because when the five-year period between our birthdays (all in the same month) between we boys occurred it instigated a change in our riding positions. Austin retained the stool with baby Vallance in Mother's lap for the whole time until Father sold it. Unfortunately, because he had a stiff leg, which made it difficult for him to drive a car, something Mother wanted, or possibly because of the expense of a growing family we did not become a car owning family.

STAMFORD FAIR

The above picture is very similar to the scene I remember when we passed through a town on the A1 on our journey to London on fathers B.S.A. motorcycle and sidecar in the 1920's. But I think the dress indicates it was some years before our time, but the man in the foreground could be using a mobile phone! (My thanks to Lincolnshire County Council: Stamford Museum for the photographs)

Our longest journey must have been when we travelled to London to spend a holiday with Grandma Evans in Camberwell about 160 miles from Burslem. It must have been an exciting day but tiring on rough roads by present standards, through many villages and I suppose at a low average speed. I vividly remember one small town because as we approached the sound of strident music indicated that a fair or Wakes was in progress. To our surprise as we entered the main street we found coconut shies with all the fairground stalls on both pavements and bunting overhead as Father drove slowly along. As the music became louder we could see the road was completely occupied by The Grand Dragons Roundabout (carousel), leaving only the straw covered pavement to pass through. Whether the larger vehicles had been diverted and Father missed the sign I don't know but a policeman directed him

46

through, with other traffic. The music reached a crescendo as we passed through the narrow opening giving the effect of escaping the Dragons careering round to the accompaniment blare from the steam driven organ with cymbals crashing. It must have tested Father's skill negotiating through the London traffic to Camberwell after his long drive over strange roads but I think with no mechanical repairs on route.

On most of our journeys picnic and toilet places were very necessary to accommodate natures call and as the 'Outrider' it became part of my duty to be on the look out for suitable spots. Within a certain radius of home some venues became favourite for our picnics with we boys, ravenous and very happy, helping to arrange the spread and after Father had managed to get the primus stove going and, providing a make shift windshield, one of us was given sentry duty to insure it kept functioning. The first cups of tea being savoured with relish providing none of the ingredients, and later, condiments or utensils had not been forgotten which sometimes added to the fun. 'Spending a penny' prior to and after the picnic was part of the routine, now called comfort stops, no problem for us but Mother being the only female who required special requirements. Location free of nettles and suitably out of sight with one or two of us keeping a sharp look out for any movement, human or vehicular, within an half a mile radius. I remember asking Mother why she didn't wear dark green underwear to blend in with the bushes and Dad suggesting that 'the full shining moon' would still be a problem.

Ensuring that our banquet area was tidy and clear of litter (always taken home) served a twofold purpose making sure no picnic utensils were hidden and that it was tidy before we left. "The grass will soon spring up again," Dad would say and the spots, which have received private ammonia treatment, will become lush and green.

The Potteries area and adjacent Derbyshire are very hilly which taxed all transport vehicles but there was one, Corkscrew Hill, I think en-route to Manifold Valley where all the family had to walk up after seeing Dad depart, running alongside Bessie in low gear, difficult with his stiff leg. Climbing some of the hills certainly made the old bike work hard but the descents taken with great care, low gear assisting the wedge type brake blocks in the vee channels, which became less effective when hot. Indeed, later I was to learn the importance of maintaining my bicycle brakes, always needed, in good working order, a smaller form of friction pads.

One could never compare Father running alongside the combination with the magnificent sight of two, three, sometimes four Shire horses with heavily loaded drays tackling the steep hills in the Potteries. Their bodies presenting a picture of power, ironclad hooves pounding the Granite covered roads with occasional sparks flying, the jingle and creak of harness. In cold weather their nostrils belched out clouds of steam and in summer a line of foamy sweat around the collar. To see the drivers walking alongside, encouraging them by name, ever watchful when to guide them to a position of rest with quick application of brakes and wheel chocks to allow them to relax from the strain of the heavy dray, often a beer wagon. Then to judge when the horses indicated they were willing to continue the battle up the hill.

It was my privilege, as a young boy, to witness those scenes many times until lorries, steam and motor, began to replace the horse-drawn transport. I wonder if the joy and aura of seeing power in motion appeals mostly to the male mind because steam railway engines fascinate boys from an early age. The sound and sight of steam with smoke above the gyrating connecting rods to the pounding coupled wheels on their steel tracks. A particular thrill was to witness the distant approach of a through express, heralding its appearance with repeated whistle blasts and passing with a roar through a station. Leaving a dying wind smelling of smoke and steam with a departing toot of thank you for standing clear and new plume of steam from the bright, green, red or black monster as it put on full power to return its retinue of carriages to full speed.

Little did I realise some fifteen years later I would be carrying out a similar duty as the drivers of horse and train but, with the assistance of other watch keeping marine engineers ensuring the powerful engines of our sea transporters, safely ploughed the oceans of the world. Also lucky to experience, with satisfaction, the thousand horse power triple expansion steam reciprocating engines with their flashing connecting rods, gyrating eccentrics rotating large exposed crankshafts connected to twenty foot diameter propellers in the stern. The sound and smells were different, but not unlike land locomotives when on the straight or horse drawn carts climbing hills. The marine engines, running smoothly in calm seas but in rough stormy weather, labouring at all angles, revolutions increasing when the stern rises and bow ships tons of sea water, drastically reducing when it lifts and propellers again grip the turbulent sea to push the ship on her way.

Also in the stokehold were seen teams of firemen showing the beauty of manpower, their gleaming perspiring bodies reflecting the red glow of roaring fires in boiler furnaces. An inspiring sight to see their skill in aiming shovels full of coal into the five foot deep fire-boxes, (high furnaces, 4ft above floor level) at the same time balancing their bodies on the ever moving floor-plates. Then to await the signal, ten or fifteen minutes later of a shovel rattling on a steel bulkhead, to open up and rake the burning coals further into the furnace, with the occasional cry, 'klinker' when a Trimmer would quench the molten mass with a bucket of sea water as it fell to the floor-plates giving off an acrid smell.

What a sight it must have been in the TITANIC, and ships of similar size, with six large stokeholds, to see dozens of men toiling twenty to thirty feet below sea level in a hot dimly lit, smoke filled, atmosphere, keeping 66,000 tons of steel ploughing the Atlantic in all it's moods.

It was after reading a book about the Titanic sinking and my five hours in the engine room and stokehold on the STUART STAR when she was lost on the rocks at East London South Africa 1937 (recorded in I SURVIVED), which gave me an inkling of the trauma the 35 engineer officers and their men must have suffered before they were drowned. They valiantly kept the lights burning only minutes before she sank.

However, leaving the 'power in motion' scenes and returning to Father awaiting us at the top of Corkscrew Hill we re-boarded Bessie brought to life with a kick start, departing with a sense of achievement something which I think is necessary for one's well being. The notorious hill was later by-passed but still presented a steep climb.

My previous reference to my Father's stiff leg must have been a liability for him in many ways. I was very young when I first noticed it, after a dog had bitten his leg, and was told that was the reason he couldn't bend his leg. It was years later when I learnt that as a young boy he had contracted Tuberculosis of the knee and an operation locked the joint. Apparently, for a time, he wore leg irons and then crutches and I was told that they did not stop him playing football with other boys' using his crutches on occasions to dribble the ball in his favour.

Little did I realise that since writing this, although a bane for his adult life, I may have lost him at an early age like thousands of children of my generation through the First World War. He did volunteer for the army, but was not accepted because of his 'gammy' leg, and I recall him saying that a number of times he was offered a white feather by thoughtless females.

To return to the motorcycling, I can only remember one instance when we were lucky not to have an accident and had to leave Bessie returning home by train. It was in open flat country, no traffic, cruising in the centre of a long straight road, when Mother, now used to bouncing along in her sidecar, called to father, "I can hear something knocking in my wheel". We pulled into the side of the road, Father using a wooden trestle he had made to support the sidecar, and to everyone's horror the wheel came off in his hand. He remarked how lucky it was with the large camber (which the roads had then) that it had not been necessary for him to drive into the gutter to allow oncoming traffic to pass, which could have caused the wheel to fly off. The combination was pushed with care to a village garage some miles away for repair, we returned home by train and Father collected it some week later.

All our excursions were an adventure, not only visiting beauty spots and places of interest, Rudyard Lake, Alton Towers, Mow cop, The Reekin, Manifold Valley with its miniature railway, Thor's Cave to name a few but the potential delay due to mechanical or tyre puncture. The latter understandable because the roads were built for horse drawn traffic, rough surfaces with many potholes. After the first year or so, Father became competent to nurture the bike's task by his driving skill and cope with any mechanical 'hiccup' from the intricacies of 'Bessie' gained from his numerous spells of maintenance in the back yard. Even punctures, mostly slow ones, caused some delay by frequent inflation stops but were repaired at home. However, there were times when a repair was necessary during the journey. The roadside became our work place, often a gateway to a field to be clear of the traffic. The affected wheel removed, carefully opening up the tyre with tyre levers and not causing additional punctures by pinching the tube. Punctures were found by detecting escaping air by cheek or mouth. The area marked with a blue pencil, roughened with emery cloth, cleaned and coated with rubber solution. A suitable patch was similarly treated after removing its protective paper and after some minutes pressing it over the hole(s). Finally sprinkling the repair with French powder and reassembly but care with those tyre levers. Often the British weather made our emergency stops challenging for dad and me in more ways than one, eventually packing away the tools and remounting onto a cold wet seat.

To know how to repair punctures from the experience gained on Father's motorcycle was to stand me in good stead later when I acquired a bicycle of my own.

EUSTON PARK – RURAL PASTIMES COUNTRY FAIR
JUNE 1998

MOUNTED ON A SIMILAR BIKE TO MY FATHER'S
80 YEARS LATER

CHAPTER SEVEN

CYCLING DAYS

My first cycle was a second-hand RENSHAW and I remember seeing it, with my Father, hanging up in a shed in a house near the Burslem Co-operative Society's, Bakery, Confectionery, Warehouse etc., and stables, which I think accommodated some forty to fifty horses and a small garage. The large site included a boot repairing works, of which my Father was the manager, where fifty cobblers, six to ten machinists with two ladies in the dispatch departments were accommodated.

The bicycle was covered in grease and accumulated dust, but when cleaned by me with enthusiasm was in excellent condition and he bought it for £2.00 with the understanding I would repay him out of my weekly pocket money. It was the standard design gentleman's bicycle but with the luxury of a Sturmy-Archer, three speed gear operated from the handle-bars and I think had 28" wheels in a 26" frame. It was a little on the large size for me but with the saddle in the lowest position I was able to reach the pedals with my heels without the need for wooden blocks, quite a common practice to enable children to ride bikes which they soon grew to suit.

Acquiring it was the beginning for me to explore places further afield and develop an interest in tinkering with things mechanical; two aspects which were to continue and expand in the years ahead.

Mending punctures was the first essential skill because most roads were flint covered in different forms, which gave a non-slip surface, but hard wearing on the tyres and an ability to pierce them when they became worn. Therefore a puncture repair outfit carried in a small case behind the saddle and pump clipped to the frame was always carried when venturing some miles distance from home. One was able to repair the tube without removing the wheel but sometimes a slow puncture, after checking the exposed tube with an open mouth, it was quicker to remove the wheel to a nearby puddle and sometimes when no water source was available, ask an inhabitant for the loan of a basin of water. Having found the leak, marked with a pencil, the area roughened with emery cloth, cleaned and coated with solution, some minutes later to allow it to dry, the patch placed firmly in position and the area covered with French chalk. Replacing the partially inflated tube in the tyre was done with care, using tyre levers not to trap the tube, and ensuring the valve stem was above the tube wires, usually the position from which to refit the tube.

The three speed Sturmy-Archer was a great benefit climbing the many steep hills in the Potteries and surrounding countryside which also meant the need for good brakes which I always maintained with care, adjustment and replacement of brake blocks. In wet weather one had to allow for their poor efficiency until the rim surfaces had dried. Many miles were covered but I derived much pleasure in cleaning and maintaining it in good working order. My Father's refusal to buy a new one proved to be good counsel because after running my Renshaw a few years, the experience in riding and maintaining it gave me valuable knowledge to care for my new Raleigh later. The Renshaw continued to give many years service to my brother Austin who acquired it and I don't recollect any payment for it.

The front cover shows the brothers Swain and their two-wheeled steeds, Austin with my old Renshaw and Vallance with Fairy Cycle, which Austin had handed down.

Buying the new Raleigh was a lesson in economics I will always remember and proved to be a 'yardstick' throughout my life. Firstly, during the years my good Renshaw was in service, my Father suggested I should save some of my pocket money in a Post Office Savings account and when the time came for me to buy a racing bike, I confidently produced £5.19s.6d for its purchase. He was with me at Alcocks, the cycle shop, and paid another £1 for a three speed gear to be fitted as a bonus for my saving ability and asked the salesman for 2½% discount for a cash transaction, which he got. Outside we discussed the savings I had made, interest from the Post Office and cash discount reducing the cost considerably, a policy I followed and still do!

CHAPTER EIGHT

GOING TO THE PICTURES

The silent pictures were a very popular form of entertainment during my childhood years and continued to attract me when a teenager. Indeed the cinema became a weekly evening out for my parents, who when I was old enough, left me in charge to look after my brothers, mostly during the winter months on Friday evenings.

There were three picture houses in Burslem, as we children called them, The Hippodrome, Palladium and Coliseum, all located in the same area. As I remember the two former were not as 'posh' as the Coliseum, which I think, may have previously been a Music Hall, having the characteristics of a theatre, circular balcony with 'boxes' adjacent to a stage with orchestra pit etc.

One sees children today eating all sorts of toffees in the street as well as huge rolls throughout the week, the former bad for the teeth and the latter contributing to early obesity. We were fortunate because most children only had sweets on Saturdays and in my case the money had to be earned for the luxury. After the Saturday morning chores, cleaning windows, chopping sticks, getting the coal in, running errands, boot black cleaning, polishing the families boots and being rewarded with 2d. A fortune, enabling one to buy, two gobstoppers, a large spherical hard sweet which changed colour as the toffee dissolved, or a liquorice stick or Kali Dab and then off to the Palladium to the Saturday afternoon 'Penny Rush' to see Tom Mix and Ruth Rolland. Knowing we would leave them in some sort of predicament and having to earn another penny next week to see what happened. Near the end of the program, an attendant walked the aisles spraying a sweet scented disinfectant to smother all sorts of smells (happenings) before the grown-ups arrived after teatime. I remember, there were no intervals as such, but the lights were put on to make sure some of the entrepreneurs among us were not hiding under the back row seats trying to extend our penny's worth into the evening's performance. Looking back one can now appreciate the skills of the lady or gentleman who provided appropriate music to suit and added emphasis to the moving picture above, from the old 'joanna' behind the curtain in front of the screen. I might add often drowned by our urgent cries "Look out he's behind you", when the villain was up to his tricks, or "Shut that door" when a draught from the lavatory caused ripples on the screen.

I was vividly reminded of the disinfecting process when Grace and I arrived at Christchurch, New Zealand via L.A. (1981) when all passengers in the aircraft were asked to remain seated until we had been carefully sprayed and dog sniffed. I believe the former to protect New Zealand's agriculture from the fruit fly and the latter, drugs. The Kiwi Islanders sensibly protective, like we used to be before the Channel Tunnel which now makes easy access for drugs etc.

CHAPTER NINE

NEWARK-ON-TRENT

My Father, the eldest of five children, one a girl, was born in Newark, educated till the age of thirteen when he had to leave school to help support the family. He had several errand boy jobs before serving a Cordwainer/shoe repairer's apprenticeship. After becoming a journeyman he met Mother in Nottingham and obtained a position with the Burslem Co-operative Society married and 'set up home' in The Potteries, Staffordshire.

Newark became my 'second home' from an early age; I think six, when I spent my first holiday with my Grandmother. I remember very clearly that first train journey, quite an adventure, because I had to change trains at Derby and Nottingham. I was put aboard at Longport Station, in those days a non-corridor carriage, with my small two part soft basket case secured with two straps and carrying handle. A label, I presume, with my name, Newark and home address on the other side, was tied to my coat with instruction how to cross over the platform, there were many at Derby, to find the Nottingham Station. Passengers in my carriage assured my parents they would see I was put off at Derby Station because I think it was a London train.

Details of the trip I have forgotten, except the difficulty of carrying my basket case and the wonderful sight of Grandma greeting me with open arms at Nottingham. I'm sure when I was posted to Grandmothers my parents knew I would be safe, the only worry being that I would not catch the Nottingham train and arrive in London. But one must reflect on how safe children were then, compared with today or perhaps the media coverage, radio and television over emphasise with repetition of the unfortunate incidents of today.

My Grandparent's house was similar to ours in The Potteries but smaller, no front garden and the backyard shared with a neighbour with facing doors. An exit to the road was shared by three more houses but all had a garden about ten yards long with outdoor 'privies' and between some accommodation for live stock, chickens, rabbits or the odd pig. Access to three bedrooms was by a staircase between the living room and parlour whose door opened directly onto the pavement. My small bedroom, with a made up bed on the floor, was entered through the grandparent's room and was over the small kitchen, with the one source of water with a stone sink. Also in the dining room there was a highly polished fireplace with a brass knob on its oven door and a tap on the boiler on the opposite side. During my first years the front bedroom was my uncle Jim's ten years older than me, the last of the children to leave home.

My recollection of my first school holidays, three/four weeks are vague, accompanying grandma shopping etc., but I do remember playing with local children playing a game called 'Snobs' with five glazed earthenware cubes, the main theme being progressively to pick up the remaining snobs whilst tossing in the air the ones on the back of the hand. Obviously with four in the air and having to grab the one off the floor catching all in the hand, was most difficult. There were further tasks with the cubes if one was successful, which I don't remember.

The environment of Newark, a market town, was a complete change to smokey Burslem and therefore to me was a real holiday. Later exploring the town and surrounding districts with mainly an agricultural atmosphere, but there were three large engineering works, Worthington & Simpson (pumps), Ransome & Marles (ball bearings) and Farr's (boiler makers). Two railways served the town, London Midland & Scottish (LMS) cross-country Nottingham to Lincoln and the London North Eastern Railway (LNER), North/South, Newcastle-on-Tyne to London and did provide employment for a large number of people. Indeed, three male members of the Swain family except my father and one brother at Ransome & Marles, worked on the LNER at one time, including my aunt's husband, all of who later provided adventures for me in their company. My grandfather was a porter, one uncle in a signal-box and for a short time the youngest in the engine sheds hoping to become an engine driver before failing an eye test, and my aunt's husband a goods yard foreman.

Vernon Street was about half a mile from the London main line and one could hear the whistle and roar of the trains passing, especially when the wind was from the east. Grandfather would habitually comment, looking at the clock or his watch, whether the passenger or goods train was on time or was running late. Often he would be wearing his railway uniform, either ready to go on duty or had returned from shift. Very familiar was the brass buttoned waistcoat with alpaca sleeves, used in summer, having two pairs of trousers with heavy overcoat for the colder weather, all supplied by the company every year (something I was to find in later years, the shipping companies never did), in those days a valuable contribution towards relieving the household expenditure but perhaps compensating for a low wage. I believe tips were expected from passengers for handling their luggage was also appreciated.

When I was allowed to play further afield, I spent many hours at the Beacon Hill Bridge watching the trains pass-by taking their names and numbers for my 'Log Book' aiming to get more than other boys, also the dubious practice of some boys putting their halfpennies on the line to make them larger and thus into pennies.

Billy Southern the Blacksmith, whose smithy was a short distance into town, in William Street, off Barnby Gate, became a 'magnet' attracting me to spend many interesting hours. At first watching at the door and soon to become part of the establishment, offering to pump the hearth fire with the long wooden arm on the large bellows. Later helping with minor jobs – being allowed to paint the hooves of the newly shod horses with an oily mixture. I suspect my many questions and being a chatterbox with a North Staffordshire accent gave me an edge on the other children wanting to get involved. I was to obtain some basic engineering knowledge from Billy whose many skills involved repairing and making a variety of farm implements for carts etc. An example was to see him measure a piece of flat steel bar, three and a seventh x the diameter, minus a very important amount for shrinkage and then bend into a ring and weld. To see the skill in heating the ring in the fire moving it continuously and putting it quickly on the wooden wheel and finally quenching with water, listening to the creaking of the spokes as they were compressed into their sockets in rim and hub.

My thanks to Mr Donald Wright Editor and Director of The Newark Advertiser for reproducing the above

At times when there were no horses to shoe and no other job to finish, he would look up at the walls with rows of iron shoes in their primary form, many sizes and obtaining a bar from the rack, then say "Stanley, we'll make some to re-stock the shortages". First, with a guillotine cut appropriate lengths and then with me at the bellows keeping the fire at the right burn, progressively form them into shape. A production line requiring his wonderful skill with the ringing sound of the anvil and hammer and with me moving three or four shoes in the fire ensuring no part burnt but was at the right heat for its next contact with the hammer. Sadly, now, the like of

Billy are few and far between. I was lucky as a boy to have smelt the burning of hooves, heard the beat of the hammer, the answering ring of the anvil and been able to have spent absorbing hours with a man of skill, knowledge and kind nature who I am pleased to report continued a busy life, later with other pursuits till his 92nd year.

Ever nosy, there was a small farm on the opposite side of the road to Billy's and when I saw a few cows being herded into sheds behind the building, I asked the man were they going to be milked? Whether I was invited or followed him in I cannot remember but soon was witnessing the cows being milked, a new experience for me. It became a short stopping off place when either visiting Billy or exploring further afield, to watch the milking. Again, perhaps my curiosity and foreign accent interested the milkman because he allowed me in the stalls and suggested if I would like to know how to milk a cow I should bend down and observe closely his busy hands. He was explaining how you gently and firmly squeeze the teats with a rhythmic one two, with me studiously seeing and hearing the milk blurp or ring on the side of the foaming pail. Suddenly, his one two became three when he dexterously jetted a stream of warm milk all over my face with accompanying loud laughter "How's that for a bull's eye christening?" It certainly was a christening, the first time I had savoured milk direct from a cow at two feet!

After a few visits I asked if I could try milking a cow, but the owner persistently refused saying that Maisie, Gerty or Annabel would not like a strange male relieving them of their nutritious milk and would try and kick me. He explained that, in general, females of all species were very particular about personal contact with the opposite sex, something I would learn when I grew up. But I was allowed to remove the head halters after milking when they would swing round leaving the stalls. However, I couldn't have been standing far enough back in the corner when one of the 'old girls' collected me between her horns, trotting out with me as a headdress. Fortunately, the milkman waiting outside quickly removed me from my mobile 'hallstand' remarking with some humour "That's a daft thing to do, neither of you can see where you are going". Needless to say after that incident my interest in cows, especially milking, waned.

Newark had two livestock markets, Tuesday for poultry, Wednesday, cows, sheep and pigs, both situated the other side of the town to Vernon Street. When I was allowed to go further afield and was able to use an old bike of my uncle's, they became a regular venue, always making a morning and sometimes a full day's attendance. There was so much to see and for me to learn about farming life first hand and sometimes able to take part. During my first years, very few animals were brought to market by lorry, some by train, the Midland Station adjacent but most driven in from the outlying farms. The farmer's staff brought some in but there was a group of 'odd job' characters that were given the task after the sales had finished of delivering them. The auctioneers' men and market employees moved the beasts during the sale and I was to witness how some were cruel, but found the stick and shouting was the only way to control them. I was not to understand then how the poor frightened beasts had already been driven many miles, from their tranquil quiet fields to a hostile, noisy, concrete floored place into small iron-railed pens with dozens of companions in a similar state. I'm sure we humans would not behave any better having been subject to a similar fate, no wonder they were frightened and difficult to

Control. Again I was pleased to see there were men who, presumably after the sale, milked some thus relieving the poor beasts whose udders were extended with milk running from their teats, obviously having missed their normal milking time perhaps purposely to show their capacity.

We young boys would watch the busy scene, sitting on the boundary wall, obtaining a good view of the sheep sales when the auctioneer moved along the pens below us, similarly the pigs, but the cattle were sold in a ring, out of bounds for us. The first and only opportunity we had to participate was when the cattle moved from the market to start the journey to their new home. We would offer our services to the drovers, very seldom accepted but would go along, and when the opportunity arose ran ahead to seal off a potential escape route for the beasts. The men let us help and on rare occasions give us a penny or two, which made us feel important and I soon got to know which drovers were generous. Often I would walk and run miles to a farm with cattle, finally returning home to grandmother ravenous and tired but what a wonderful day spent in the fresh air and learning more about the people of the countryside.

I learned to swim at Newark, in the river at the 'bathing place'. There was no covered in swimming pool which Burslem had, open all year round, heated chlorinated water in two pools, a shallow one for children. Also public bathrooms and laundry facilities were used as very few houses had bathrooms or were able to heat large quantities of water. We at home used a galvanised bath which hung outside in the yard, brought in Friday night and the 'copper' (coal fired boiler) for hot water.

The Bathing Place at Newark was located on the north side of the river, a primitive arrangement, a concrete quay, open dressing cubicles with a platform across the water and wooden poles slung at water level about twenty five yards downstream. The attendant, I think his name was Sam Taylor, was a dedicated man and had to be very vigilant because there was quite a flow of water, especially when the mill was not working on Saturday afternoons because the Bathing Place was on the course of the river, but there were two branches off upstream, one to the mill and the other a 'locked' canal that passed the castle. When the large water mill was working much of the river's flow was diverted, the water returned to the river some distance down stream, thereby reducing the flow at the Bathing Place. Very few boys could swim against the current, everyone relying on grabbing the poles downstream and then, hand over hand, back to the quay steps. Non swimmers had to use water wings, I think made from linen because they had to be soaked to make them water tight before inflation then tied with tapes under the arms. All learners were individually taught by Sam who fastened a harness with a hook around the chest and then with a long bamboo pole hooked onto the harness allowed the beginner to float down the river, retrieving them back to terra firma before un-hooking.

Instructions on breathing, the use of arms and legs on the 'voyage' was given during the breath-taking first trip and a limited number of 'goes' because the water was never warm. Strict instructions and inspection afterwards to dry thoroughly and dress quickly was the 'order of the day'. Depending upon the pupils progress, swimming with the pole continued. Eventually without water wings, secretly, Sam would un-hook, and after a number of times would tell you, to your surprise, "You can swim now". He would monitor further trips until the pupil was completely confident because the water was many feet deep. I do remember my first swim in the Burslem baths and found it difficult, seeming to require more energy, perhaps because of the 'hard water' and absence of river flow.

My introduction to Howard's, the corn merchants, was by a neighbour of my grandparents, Mr Wakefield, a horseman who drove one of their drays. Probably when I admired his horse when he sometimes came home for a meal. Prince was a large, brown, most likely shire, and eventually I was taken for a ride, returning to Howard's Mill where the horses were stabled.

The mill became another place of interest, situated near Vernon Street, four stories high, a gas engine on the ground floor, which had to be started to operate the sack hoist and other machinery. Always an interesting sight to see the grain sacks quickly linked with the chain and hoisted to the top floor and swung in where it was stored. There, they would be emptied through trap doors into hoppers, from which it could be ground, rolled or mixed, finally bagged awaiting delivery on the first floor. The middle floors were out of bounds but I was shown, on the top floor, mice scurrying away, sometimes from their nests when the sacks were moved, the first time I had seen their young, pink, bare bodies.

Riding and seeing the good delivered, sometimes coal on the drays or carts was great fun and , when older, giving a helping hand. Mid-day Saturday was a special treat by riding the led horses to the fields and when released showed their pleasure with tossing of heads and frisky trot to savour the grass and knowing they had a restful time ahead.

My pleasure riding and working with the horses was somewhat diminished when I had a painful experience in the railway goods yard. Both railway stations were on the outskirts of the town, the 'Midland' (LMS) on the north side near the castle and cattle market but the 'Northern' (LNER), some distance away on the east side. Presumably to give a service nearer the town centre the 'Northern' had a branch line to a small goods yard terminating at Barnby Gate. The single line track after passing Blagg & Johnson's crossed over Massey Street behind the Maltings. At one time two tracks in the siding accommodated trucks, with a loading and unloading area, in between an office and weighbridge, with my uncle Benjamin being the yard foreman. The goods yard was a familiar place to me due to the many time either grain or coal was collected by Mr. Wakefield needless to say part of the enjoyment riding with him was to help with the chores when allowed to do so.

On this occasion I was leading Prince around in a tight arc across the yard when he trod on my foot. Fortunately he was pulling an empty dray, consequently not supporting any extra to his weight (a few cwts.). Luckily he continued to walk on but it seemed ages with me laying on the floor trapped, watching and waiting for his three other legs to move until he lifted his iron shod hoof from my very paintful toe. As I remember, after removing my shoe, (plimsolls) the big toe was badly bruised, but no broke skin but my carting activities cut short. Indeed the toe was painful for some time afterwards but no medical treatment required. However, to this day I have carried a reminder of the incident with a discoloured toenail.

It was during my visits I got to know Herbert, who drove the Chevelet lorry for Howards. Motor transport was beginning to replace horses and were a novelty to ride in, much sort after by youngsters. When I was a little older and possibly able to help, Herbert invited me to accompany him, which provided me with adventures further afield. I was really excited when he suggested I could go with him, Grandma permitting, to distribute coal to customers in the Muskham Village district some miles north of Newark. Two ten-ton railway wagons would be in the village sidings, off the main L.N.E. Railway line. Having got the all clear from Grandma, I was up early, cutting 'doorstep sandwiches' with an extra large slice of cake and fruit, quickly cycling to the yard to join my 'Driver'. It was a beautiful summer's day, soon arriving at Muskham to see, to me the huge wagons, one with large and the other filled with smaller coal. The first job was to dig out coal from the wagon door, enabling it to be opened and the lorry brought alongside. All the coal shovelled, the bulk delivered direct into the lorry and weighed on the siding weigh bridge, the rest bagged into one hundredweight sacks, using a machine we had brought with us.

It was hard dirty work, but for me it was an experience, delivering to country people their fuel for the coming winter. Meeting a varied cross section from large farmers to young and old housewives in cottages. The former sometimes told us to dump the coal in the yard the old ladies requiring it to be carried into small sheds near their back doors. Interestingly, the latter often supplying refreshment and the odd pensioner giving me a coin in appreciation of the service.

By the end of the first day, there were more orders to fulfil requiring a second day's visit to the sidings. My arrival home, happy, hungry and tired but dirty was greeted by grandmother with concern and jokingly said, "I think the best thing to do is to take your shoes off and get into a tub of hot water, I'll be able to clean you and your clothes in one go". I told her I would like to return, while she took my clothes down the garden and after a good shaking, returning them with instructions to dress in the kitchen in the morning. I undressed in the back kitchen and washed 'piecemeal' in a small tub. In my pyjamas I enjoyed a good tuck in gratefully retired to a no-stop sleep until I was making more 'doorstep sandwiches' the next morning.

Meeting Herbert, he was surprised I was allowed to return and remarked, "You have a good grandma, she believes in finishing a job", to which I said "Yes, and that will be when I'm in a tub of hot water with my clothes on"! Little did I think I would again be shovelling coal, years later, learning to fire marine boilers.

An adventure which is still so clear in my mind today, but very traumatic at the time proved to be a good lesson for my future behaviour. I was friendly with another boy of my age who lived in Vernon Street, and we explored the countryside together on our bicycles. There were a number of estates surrounding Newark and on this particular day we noticed some small fir trees in a large plantation. We both thought it would be a good idea to take one home for the garden and hopped over the wire netting both of us uprooting a small tree. We fastened them to the crossbars of our cycles and shortly afterwards, some distance away from the plantation, decided to eat our sandwiches laying our bikes on the grass verge. We were enjoying our picnic when a man passed on his cycle but stopped and walked back and asked us where we had obtained our trees. It transpired that he was a Game Keeper and explained that a lot of trees were being stolen lately, while escorting two very worried boys some distance to his cottage. There he told us he must report us to the Estate Manager but was a kindly man offering us an apple while we waited. Needless to say we declined, we were in no mood for feasting. He added that on occasions when he had caught boys 'scrumping' his apples he put them in his shed and told them they would be released only when they had eaten all they had stolen. He added that one young man whom he had caught some years before, told him that since that day he was never keen on apples and never drank cider. After relieving us of the trees, he took our names and addresses and told us to report on Saturday morning to the Estate Office. We certainly were two very worried boys riding home full of apprehension when Grandma and my friend's parents knew of our downfall.

Our news was certainly received with a severe scolding but greater concern on what the outcome of the office visit would be. I certainly suffered during the few days awaiting 'Black Saturday' when accompanied by my Uncle Tom we cycled to the village and entered the Estate Office. I can still remember the stern, bald-headed gentleman seated behind a large desk with the Game Keeper standing beside him and the severe 'dressing down' he gave us. We were dismissed, both in tears, whilst he considered his verdict, Uncle Tom staying behind. It seemed ages before we were told to return where a further reprimand was given but told on this occasion there would be no further punishment and after promising never to steal again we departed with great relief.

Later I learned that the Estate Manager could see we were not the real culprits who were stealing large numbers of young trees for sale. My Uncle Tom's presence must have helped considerably, not only establishing our comparative innocence but by coincidence, during the War, he had served in the same Scottish Regiment as the Manager and would ensure the lesson would be 'hammered home'. Indeed, I know in my case it was never forgotten particularly as my further worry had been my Father's reaction when he learnt of my misdemeanour. I often wondered whether he was ever told?

My brother, Austin, spent little time at Newark but I know he will well remember the weekend visit the family made to attend my Uncle Jim's wedding at Balderton. I would have been 14/15, he being five years younger, when we were released from the wedding proceedings to amuse ourselves.

On a borrowed bike, with him on the crossbar, I took him for a tour showing him some of my haunts, one being the old swimming pool on the millrace where I was taught to swim by Sam Taylor. Returning homewards along the towpath I decided there was sufficient room to ride through the gap between a pair of 'kissing gates', to save dismounting. My judgement was ok, but unfortunately the handlebars touched the post diverting our course into the river. This produced a shocked teenager with a non-swimming brother, in their 'best suits' and bicycle disappearing into the muddy River Trent. My first reaction was to retrieve Austin and with difficulty, treading water, I helped him to mount the 2/3 foot high bank, after which I dived down to retrieve the bike buried in the muddy bottom.

Suffice to say our reception at 45 Vernon Street was of great concern to all hands because it was cold weather but short bursts of running with the bike had kept our 'central heating' going. However, I was not happy to say the least because I was expecting a broadside from my Father but was much relieved when he commented that I had got my priorities right, by rescuing Austin before the bike. During the rescue operation retrieving Austin and the bike from the river, two young ladies walked past witnessing, what we though was an unusual event, but Austin remarked afterwards that they continued walking past not even looking at our muddy figures and bike, saying "It must be a common occurrence".

The journey home on Sunday in borrowed clothes provided an unforgettable time. Austin was rigged out in a cousin's clothes, a boy of similar age, but I was fixed up with my Uncle Jim's brass buttoned blue blazer and grey 'Oxford Bags', much too big for me. I recollect the trousers were fastened well above my 'belly button'. My uncle, at that time being a young man, not quite a Dandy, but certainly dressing in the height of fashion, therefore my appearance in the ill-fitting rig caused a great pantomime in the family circle. Indeed the train journey home must have caused surreptitious glances from some passengers, seeing a too large debonair outfit on a schoolboy. I remember brother Austin remarking with some emphasis the single word 'TRENT' when we stopped at the Trent Railway Station before reaching Nottingham, which greatly amused our parents.

NEWARK-ON-TRENT

MARKET PLACE 1920's

NEWARK CASTLE

GRANDMOTHER AND ME AT THE
BACKDOOR AT VERNON STREET

NEWARK TOWN HALL

MARKET PLACE 2000

CHAPTER TEN

RAILWAY ADVENTURES

One of my Grandfather's overtime duties on the L.N.E. Railway was to clean and replenish the oil lamps used on the signals. It was a fortnightly job and he was able to take me with him when I was old enough. A treat to walk along the main lines, experiencing a real thrill, close to those beautiful shining, powerful engines as they passed. Southbound, gathering speed after stopping at Newark Station amid clouds of steam and smoke, the rhythm of escaping steam and clanking connecting rods, gradually accelerating, compared with the through expresses roar with shrill whistle to keep well clear. The north bound expresses warning of their approach at speed and the stopping trains slowing down with squealing brake-shoes, sparks flying off them.

So many things going on to interest a young boy, the stuttering clatter of wagon buffers, greeting a new arrival to their train from the shunting engine, a fussy small tank engine. Opposite to the goods yard were the engine sheds another scene of work, many engines being serviced, cleaned, replenished with water and coal, in the sheds mechanical adjustment made to the engines complicated machinery, worn parts replaced. I was later able to visit the engine sheds when my Uncle Jim was training to become a fireman.

A small black hut alongside the main line, on the opposite side to the engine sheds stood the lamp workshop, having a metal covered bench, drums of Colza Oil, cleaning materials and racks with spare lamps, hung on with their hooked handles. Years later I was to see Colza (rape oil) used for the stand-by navigation lights, if the electrics failed, on ships' on which I sailed and understood it gave a brighter smokeless light than paraffin.

It was strenuous work carrying the heavy lamps to and from the signals, even to the 'Home' signals but a considerable walk to the 'Distant' gantries. Some of the signals were very high to enable engine drivers to see them above road bridges, which entailed a long vertical climb up an iron ladder, carrying and removing the lamps. I was not allowed to help but no doubt kept grandfather busy answering questions about all the activity going on around. I believe he serviced signals controlling a section of lines called a 'block', quite a responsible job, the lamps burning continuously for a week, demanding careful attention to cleaning, trimming and adjustment to the wick etc.

He told me during foggy weather he was on duty for long spells on the Edinburgh-London route, by selected signals clipping detonators on the lines whilst the signals were on danger, one could hear the explosion for some distance when the train sometimes overran the signal. It must have been cold, lonely, dreary work, but most important for safety, and sometimes I think, 'sentry' type box with coal brazier was available to give some protection, but having to be alert at all times, especially criss-crossing the rails to remove or replace detonators, a duty which helped to keep trains running albeit with some delay.

Grandfather must have spent much of his time working on the railway indeed even at home, particularly when the wind was from the east; he noted the sound of passing trains with the inevitable remark whether it was on time or minutes late after looking at his watch. Most of his spare time was spent within the sound of railway traffic because he had an allotment alongside the station that provided fruit and vegetables for the family and during my father's childhood (five children), must have been very necessary providing food to supplement his low wage. There were many allotments; most of substantial size with small huts and granddad's had a well, quite deep. His felt covered hut with many coats of tar most probably served as his second home besides a store for his gardening tools. It became a frequent place for me to visit spending some time helping to harvest the crop especially the fruit, loganberries, raspberries and late strawberries, sampling when granddad wasn't looking. Also learning a little about gardening, always to clean tools and rub with an oily rag after use, no rusty implements in his shed and frogs in the well indicated the water wasn't stagnant. Many times before he left home for duty at the station, Grandma would give him her requirements for vegetables/fruit, which often was modified according to which were ready or near the end of their season. I have often heard it said that fresh vegetable are nutritious so we certainly derived maximum benefit; ours cooked within the hour of being harvested.

Uncle Tom's Signal Box

When I was older, I was able to accompany Uncle Tom, a signalman, on one of his duty periods in the Trent signal box situated north of Newark Station. Cycling and walking alongside the tracks over the River Trent, seeing the river far below through lattice steel girders from our walkway was an experience in itself. Before we reached the signal box, passing the water troughs half a mile long between the lines which were kept full by a small pumping station, most probably using water from the river. Later in the day I was to see the spectacular sight of long distant express engines at speed lowering their scoops, which must have required critical timing topping up their water tanks, often overflowing before the scoop was lifted. One wonders whether passengers were warned because it must have created quite a noise and any youngsters with their heads out of the window a christening in cold water 'laced' with coal dust, the leading carriages receiving the full benefit.

There were other benefits we had to take care of whilst cycling to and from his signal box, the well used path was close to the track so we moved well away, sometimes lifting our bikes over the signal control wires, standing well back, especially from the passenger trains, otherwise you may have been 'anointed'. Uncle reminded me of the notices on the toilets 'Please do not use in the stations', emphasising that their use was popular before and after leaving Newark Station. He told me that the platelayers, inspection and maintenance men's job weren't embellished when corridor coaches with toilets were introduced, but the wild flowers flourished.

A signalman's job was a responsible position, higher grades in the large boxes, usually at stations controlling train movement on sidings as well as main line. The Trent box, a small one with a 'netty' (toilet) just outside the door at the top of the stairway, was a familiar sight in the country. Inside it's line of inclined signal and track changeover point levers facing the track with telegraph control boxes above. The control boxes being the 'heart' of the safety system, their tinkling pointers moved over to line clear or occupied. They were answered by signal men in 'blocks' each side of the Trent section by special signals on the bell being accepted or rejected by my uncle who would return an appropriate signal by moving the handles on his line indicator. There was also a telephone, regularly used when changes in schedule or instructions for goods trains to be allowed on or taken off the main lines, giving preference to passenger traffic. All movements logged in a ledger with relevant notes, requiring an alert mind and muscle power to pull off the distant signals. I was not allowed to move from my corner or touch a thing especially during periods of operation but the eight hour shift passed too quickly there was so much to see from my elevated position. In the far distance a tiny dot quickly growing into a beautiful monster of smoke and steam roaring past below having been heralded with the 'clickerty click' on the rails, and disappearing into the distance with a diminishing 'clackerty clack'.

The goods trains so different, in view much longer and chuffing by with clanking connecting rods hauling so many trucks with sufficient time for the engine crew to wave which appeared to me an acknowledgement to my uncle for allowing them on the main line again after waiting in one of the siding tracks, each side of the main line. Sometimes a verbal exchange through the sliding windows of his box on how long they had to reach Newark or next sidings south, before being shunted off the main line again to wait for their next 'privileged' run.

Goods trains demanded different skills to the express drivers and guards, starting, stopping and shunting a 900/1000 ton train of trucks with only the engine and guards-van brakes, must have required experience. Too much braking on either engine or van to avoid locking the wheels which wore flats on the tyres and careful starting, gradually taking up the strain to avoid breaking coupling links, easily done needing quick action if a train was on a gradient.

For me, there were two highlights on the two to ten shift, to see the Flying Scotsman train, occasionally pulled by the Flying Scotsman Engine, roaring past a twenty minutes past four. Later becoming non-stop, the engine tenders had a tunnel through for the two crews to change over into rest accommodation in the leading carriage. The second was the first of the express fish trains from Scotland passing through at speed to be in London for the early morning fish market. The wagons had coupling and vacuum-brakes the same as the passenger coaches but with other facilities to carry ice covered fish, enabling them to travel at speed, characteristically leaving in their wake a smell of fish and damp track from melting ice.

THE FLYING SCOTSMAN

CHAPTER ELEVEN

THEATRE ROYAL HANLEY – TOMMY HANDLEY

In 1930 I left Burslem Central Boys' school and for a short time was an errand boy at Warwich Savage's, a printers in Burslem. It was then arranged for me to serve a five year apprenticeship in electrical and mechanical engineering at T.M. Birket & Sons, Brass Founders and Engineers, Hanley, Stoke-on-Trent.

My relationship with the Theatre Royal, Hanley, began when I used the stage door on some Saturday nights, to watch the show from the switchboard, back stage!

The Birket brothers, Arthur, Norman and Eddie were financially connected with a number of enterprises in Stoke-on-Trent. Arthur, the eldest, resided in, I think it was called The Waverley Hotel, which he owned, in a street off the top of Hanley Market Square. He had an interest in the Theatre Royal, the Palace Cinemar/Roller Skating Rink (at one time a Boxing Arena) and the Sun Street Greyhound Track.

As all the above establishments required many kilowatts of electricity, DC generation with diesel engines had been installed, no doubt, because of the financial benefits derived from private electricity generation. Generators were put in the latter two establishments during my apprenticeship days (1931/37).

The stage lighting with front of house spots and arc lamps in the wings for the theatre entailed a large electrical load, which was supplied by two single cylinder diesel engines similar to but of smaller HP than the twin shown on page one in my book, I SURVIVED. The maintenance and efficient operation of these engines was the responsibility of Harold Wright, the Chief Engineer (my chief) of T.M. Birket & Sons, Engineering Works, Hanley. Consequently, I was involved many times in that category. So young Swain, as a wide-eyed teenager, was able to watch the Saturday night shows from the switchboard in the wings about ten feet above stage level, the privilege given as 'perks' for his labours on the engines. Needless to say I was serving another kind of apprenticeship because the theatrical life was a world much removed from my sheltered home life and at some of the shows my eyes popped out like 'organ stops'!

The switchboard controlled many battens of lights each containing 30 – 40 sixty-watt bulbs, portable floods, foot-lights and 'limes' (large carbon arc lamps) one on the switchboard and another similarly placed on the opposite side of the stage. At the time I thought the latter derived the name from the colour of the beam, but later found that originally a brilliant light was produced by heating lime with a gas flame. The heat back-stage was substantial, no wonder the artistes perspired in the summer months. Dimming of the various circuits was obtained by water resistors, 3ft deep porcelain pots filled with water into which lead cones were lowered, the lights becoming brighter as they sank deeper. When many pots were in use, sometimes for long periods, the steam generated gave the atmosphere around the switchboard the appearance of a 'Chinese Laundry'. All in all my view of the stage from an uncomfortable position was limited but was exciting at times.

My Saturday night visits enabled me to learn some of the switching operations and invariably I was called on to assist. Due to the heat etc., when the interval arrived an abnormal thirst was quenched by a mad dash through the stage door to the pub opposite. One night when Tommy Handley was 'Top of the Bill' just before the interval, the switchboard attendant asked me to take over so that he could get a head start on his thirst quenching session (I hadn't acquired a taste for beer then.) Tommy Handley was the last turn before the interval performing on a full bright stage ending with a saucy joke on a critically timed black-out. "It's simple (I was instructed by the switchboard man) just pull the master switch with one hand and push the shutter over the lime with the other". He then disappeared down the ladder with me apprehensively awaiting the all-important signal from the Stage Manager below. Off went the electrical buzzer; I pulled out the master switch tapping hard the sliding shutter. This was immediately followed by a loud clatter as it landed on the stage floor below with Tommy glaring up at my solitary spot beam with an unprintable oath. I wasn't aware that there was no stop at the end of the slide! I switched off the arc lamp, watching Tommy stalking off into the wings in its dying glow. There was a storm of applause but whether it was augmented by my 'clanger' I never knew, but certainly the timing was 'spot on'! At least I was allowed to continue my visits but I expect the SB man wasn't complimented!

Wilfred Ellis, the Stage Manager, was thankful that the heavy iron shutter did not hit anyone. He was a pleasant man and one wonders how present day stage managers would react if they were expected to be responsible for the operation of a power plant in addition to their normal duties. The work was intensive and the time consuming job of changing the colour of the lamp battens for the incoming show had to be completed on time for the Monday evening's performance. Changing the glass changed some of the batten colours but others required removing the lamps covered with a gelatine coat, which had to be dipped into a solution to remove it, and recovered with the new colour. Sometimes dozens of lamps were altered. At the time I went to sea (1937), Strand Electric Co. were replacing the whole DC system with modern equipment requiring much less power etc, and a small control console in the balcony was able to provide many scenic effects, which replaced the old equipment and switchboard.

I believe the SENTINEL on the same street as the GRAND had it's own diesel generators supplying power to the long, large, noisy printing presses with many rollers and I recall seeing them just below pavement level. One wonders whether the noise levels from the engines and printing presses ever created a problem for the audiences in the nearby theatres.

One further highlight of my visits backstage was the week an exotic programme showing nude ladies in static poses was booked for the theatre.

For some time it had been 'performed' at The Windmill Theatre in London with Jimmy Edwards and his pals. One could imagine the excitement the Theatre Royal's forthcoming programme caused in the Potteries and in particular for teenager Swain. Looking back, I do not recall my parents indicating any concern, perhaps Mother was not aware that her boy was being exposed to the lure of females but I guess Father was on the ball.

Needless to say, I was ahead of schedule on my Saturday night's attendance on the 'Red Letter Week', speeding to my switchboard perch. I was greeted with 'You're early Stanley, and you look a little excited', by the switchboard man, 'Something tickled your fancy?' 'Nothing really,' I replied. Strangely I cannot remember what the supporting acts were but soon after the interval the activity backstage, from my point of view, began to take on a disappointing element. Black drapes supported on suitable frames were put in place on each side and the back of the stage with a covering ceiling thus completely screening the fair ladies from anyone backstage. The switchboard man must have been highly amused watching my disappointment build up to a despondent early farewell, leaving well before the end of the programme.

It would be some years later when my innocence would be exposed and in a far away place, a somewhat more exotic venue than backstage Theatre Royal, Harley!

Theatre Royals' diesel engines similar to these

CHAPTER TWELVE

SUN STREET GREYHOUND TRACK

I well remember the day the two to three ton railway type bogie arrived at our workshop. It had four flanged wheels, similar in size to the five-ton trucks used on the railways in the 1930's, but the frame had no body. A 50HP DC motor, slung between the wheels, picked up its supply from a copper slipper mounted underneath. The drive to the wheels was through two heavy bevel wheel gearboxes.

It had been delivered for overhaul mainly for attention to the motor, commutator skimming etc. When I enquired of Archie Leslie, who was responsible for my apprenticeship training, what the bogie was used for, he said, "It carries the decoy hare for the Sun Street Greyhound Track". As a young, cheeky, immature apprentice and having suffered many 'leg-pulls' during my eighteen month service, I treated his remark with disdain, but when he produced a dummy hare on the end of a light ¾" tubular pole which when attached to the bogie projected some five to six feet from the side, I had to humbly apologise. It seemed ridiculous that this huge trolley was necessary just to carry a hare only a few ounces in weight to lure greyhounds round a track.

However, it transpired that there were two bogies (one spare) which ran around the outer edge of the track on railway lines under a wooden cover. Apparently, as greyhounds run at thirty mph plus, it was necessary for the hare to accelerate round the bends in order to keep well ahead of the pack and not entice the leading hound away from the inboard rail causing the rest to overtake, something the controller had to avoid at all costs. Otherwise the punters would have been 'after his blood' for 'pulling the race'. Therefore, speeds of up to sixty mph were required at times. Whether or not the high speeds were the reason, occasional derailments occurred at speed with much damage, which meant the meeting had to be abandoned. Punter casualties were never reported but I surmise the areas where the crashes took place, probably the bends, were given a wide berth. To me, witnessing such an event, would have been more exciting than watching a normal race. I wondered whether the hounds continued around the track or attacked the dummy hare amid the debris of splintered wood and crashed bogie, possibly still alive at 230 volts. Furthermore, catching the excited, frustrated dogs and keeping them apart after a normal race was no easy task for the stewards but retrieving them after a crash must have been 'summat ter sae'!

I understood, when derailments occurred, that customers were only given a free ticket for the next meeting if less than half the races had been run. However, derailments, attributed to track movement, became more frequent. This was thought to be due to subsidence, a common occurrence in North Staffordshire from mining, even though rail alignment checks were made before meetings. Also it was said the site had been a marl pit filled previously with rubbish from the 'potbanks' (pottery manufacturers). With the loss of revenue and, more important, customer satisfaction, management approached Mr. Harold Wright (Chief Engineer, T.M. Birkets) for a solution.

My first intimation that his inventive mind had been at work was when he asked me to find an old 12v starter motor from the garage. He told me to remove the Bendix drive and firmly secure the motor in a bench vice, then attach a 25lb scale weight with cable to the shaft with the weight on the floor. Then he ordered me to energise the motor from a 12v accumulator. The result was startling: the weight flew up to the vice with speed and force. "Some power there" he remarked and from then on I was involved with designing and building a small trolley with four wheels to run on a 6" x 1/8" flat rail mounted vertically with the starter motor providing the drive. The aluminium plate with four grooved wheels straddled the rail's top and bottom edges, thus captive on the rail. The motors' drive wheel, with rubber insert, engaged with the top edge of the rail and the conduit, which carried the hare, was fitted at right angles to the plate.

The following weeks proved to be a very interesting period in which prototype trolleys weighing only 20/30lbs were tested on a sample track 30ft long in the workshop yard. Two copper wires (overhead tram wires) alongside the track provided, through copper slippers, the 12v supply. Many modifications were found necessary when speed, acceleration etc., were checked within the limitations on the test track. Suitable drive arrangements and cooling ducts for the starter motor were designed. Eventually a trolley was demonstrated which gave the greyhound track management the confidence to install the 12v trolley during the few weeks closed period in the summer knowing that it had to succeed.

Installing the monorail with copper wires three feet above and in the existing track was a considerable task in time and materials. Fortunately the original direct current supply with voltage reduction and the water tank speed controller were suitable for the new hare. The first trial runs were anxious times but proved completely reliable when a new heavy-duty motor with cooling ducts was fitted. At the time and since, I was filled with admiration for Harold Wright's inventive talent and courage to install an innovative and untried system. The Harold Wright hare proved to be completely successful, cheap to manufacture, could not derail and was easy to maintain. I believe a Sumner Hare (a continuous wire rope system) became available later and eventually replaced it.

There were two other periods when my apprenticeship training contributed to interesting projects at Sun Street.

When the first electric totalizator was installed at the track it created quite a stir. The tall tower with hundreds of bulbs providing numeric indication of the bets and race dividend was a sight to be seen. However, it had only been in operation a few weeks when a fault in the equipment resulted in some happy punters receiving ten times the correct winnings because of a decimal point error. Management immediately employed staff to quickly check all calculations before payouts were displayed on the tote. In the meantime a system of checking the equipment (mechanical/electric multiple switches, similar to those at the time used in telephone exchanges) was implemented and part of my duties was to check suspect units. It was an exacting and tedious job cleaning and adjusting many finger contacts to a thousandth part of an inch.

The other project was the installation of a diesel-generating unit. Many firms, whose electricity requirements had rapidly increased in the 30's, found the public electricity supply (Corporation) unit costs expensive, power 2d, lighting 5d, when company owned diesel generation was ¾d per unit. My contribution was to design and build the distribution switchboard for the generating set. The job gave me the opportunity to design and make an angle iron framework with 'Sintdanio' panels (a new insulating composition much lighter than heavy 1½" slate slabs), carrying the many meters and copper knife switches. Copper busbars with a connecting network of bars and cables to many circuits were made and fitted behind the panels. The job required design and practical experience to make, under supervision, an apprenticeship training which proved to be a valuable asset during my working life. Sadly today, similar training has practically disappeared which in my view will affect the long-term prosperity of the United Kingdom.

CHAPTER THIRTEEN

A PALACE OF VARIETY

I am not sure what the name of the Hanley Palace, Skating and Cinema Hall was originally, but I think it was called Palais de Danse; my first recollection of its existence was as a Boxing Arena. There must have been other functions besides the boxing and it would be interesting to know for what it was originally built?

I think the first time I spent some time inside was when a group of disabled ladies, including an aunt of mine, were demonstrating the art of making artificial flowers. They were from 'John Groom's Crippleage', Sekforde Street, London E.C. This organisation now John Groom's Association for the Disabled, is still in existence today helping men and women to live fulfilled lives in specially designed flats and bungalows. Recently an Inter-city, 125 train was named 'John Groom' and bears the Disabled Logo in recognition of their valuable service to the community.

After spending some time admiring the skill of the flower makers and perhaps as a young boy, my interest was taken up with the size of the spacious hall with its huge lattice constructed transverse wooden arches supporting the roof. It was, I think, over 150 feet long and the large span of the arches provided a wide clear space with no intrusion of support columns. I was impressed with the halls structure.

During my apprenticeship at T.M. Birketts, I was involved mainly on errands when it was being converted into a roller skating rink. My chief, Mr Harold Wright, was responsible for the installation of the 'Panotrope' a broadcast system. Many powerful speakers with large, sound reflecting boards were necessary so the skaters could hear the music above the noise level produced by their rollers on the maple floor.

During my visits, I always found time to watch the craftsmen installing the maple floor with its hundreds of blocks which had to conform to an exacting pattern and was supported on an arrangement of springs underneath.

Some time later, T.M. Birketts were again involved when a diesel generator was installed to provide cheap electricity, when the hall's function was changed to a cinema.

Most existing halls converted to cinemas were small in length as originally built for theatre use, but the Palace required the largest Kalee film projectors in order to give a clear picture on the screen 150ft from the projector which was further impaired by tobacco smoke when the film attracted large audiences (rear screen projection was impractical). Direct current electricity required for the carbon arc projectors was supplied through Mercury Arc Rectifiers from the 'Corporation' but private generation provided an attractive cost saving for the large currents required by the projectors etc.

At the period when a high speed generating set was installed in a sound proof building outside the Palace, I was employed with the design and manufacture of its switchboard. A special exhaust silencer arrangement was fitted to reduce the noise level to an acceptable limit in a town centre. Unfortunately, after some weeks of satisfactory operation, complaints were received from an architect's office across the road because vibration from the engine was being transmitted to their buildings. It was discovered that the bed of the engine was on a strata of rock on which the building opposite were built. However, a costly remedial job cured the problem by isolating the engine bed on a vibration absorbent pad.

Later that year, I was to experience an interesting fortnight, when I substituted for the fourth projectionist while he was on summer holiday. My training was minimal, half an hour before an afternoon matinee, and mainly as the rewind boy. A simple time consuming job but requiring a skill, to check by sight and feel between thumb and finger as the film passed to detect whether any damage to perforations, joints etc. had occurred requiring repair. A film break was a potential fire hazard, therefore very strict fire precautions were observed because celluloid film in use then was highly inflammable when adjacent to and passing through a potential firebox.

There were three main projectors, two in use, one on standby plus a slide and colour effects projector. One spool on average carried 20-30 minutes of film and the sequence of spool change was always carefully checked. It had been known for audiences to be bemused and shocked when an endearing child of tender years was shown before the church wedding. Nowadays, such episodes appear when the sequence is correct!

The heat in the projection room was considerable due to the large powered projectors. Ventilation was minimal to prevent dust intrusion in the small iron shuttered fireproof room, which meant the operators were lightly clad and really suffered when two machines were running during changeover. Quite an important time, requiring full concentration by both operators to minimize disruption to picture and sound for the audience. Changeover points were arranged where episodes in the film altered but often this was not possible split second timing by the projectionists was essential. The incoming machine with film laced and carbon arc operating, both operators looking at the screen to see the first mark in the top corner of the picture, with the shout, 'Motor' to start the incoming projector and seconds afterwards 'Over' when the second mark appeared and the coupled shutter wire pulled simultaneously with the sound controllers.

When I was told about my 'stand in duty' I thought a bonus would be to see and enjoy the film show but as rewind boy I only had brief spells in the projector room to peep through the observation apertures. Even during the second week when I was able to run a projector, I was always occupied with the rewind and getting my machine ready, so certain sequences of the feature film I never saw.

My other lasting memory of the Palace was when, as a teenager, I saw a film on Venereal diseases, shown to separate male and female audiences (over 18). The shock of that film was to provide me with a sound protective barrier later, when I went to sea and my curiosity led me into some exciting and dangerous areas of ports worldwide. One wonders if similar educational films would still provide benefit for today's young fertile minds and bodies.

CHAPTER FOURTEEN

NORFOLK BROADS

Our forays rambling and cycling in Derbyshire and other areas around Stoke-on-Trent provided we teenagers with a modicum of adventure and exploration So when two of my work friends suggested a holiday on the Norfolk Broads, manning a hired motorboat its appeal was very attractive, provided we could afford it.

Henry Rowe and Stanley White were assistant chemists in the 'works' laboratory and when we found we could save sufficient money for the travel to Norfolk and a fortnight on the Broads it was booked with enthusiasm. We decided that each would have a main responsibility as crew member, Stanley, responsible for stores and financial departments (Chief Steward), Henry would do the cooking (Chief Cook) and I was in charge of the engine (Chief Engineer).

The planning and weeks of looking forward to the holiday provided much pleasure and lively discussion, but shortly before we were due to depart Stanley had to forego his holiday due to some domestic reason. A great disappointment to us all. However, Henry and I departed eastwards by train, which was an adventure in itself, having to change at Derby and I think Peterborough, travel by train cross country, never easy.

We arrived at Wroxham and with a little trepidation boarded our vessel and were given a short trip with the owner who demonstrated the many points we must observe so that no damage was done to his boat. I don't think we had to provide an insurance fee. We were then given the control of the boat, manoeuvring it to his instructions after which we returned to his boat yard and given an inventory to sign, which listed the many items we would be responsible to replace if lost or damaged. We carefully checked the list but were puzzled what a 'Quant' was and because the long wooden pole was the only item left our nautical knowledge was improved. He particularly emphasised extra care when leaving and coming alongside riverbanks or quays when serious damage to the wooden hull could occur. When he departed he advised us where we could get our provisions, which was a long wooden shed owned by ROYS, which may have been their first shop. ROYS today is a large and prosperous retail business.

Carefully we left the Kings Boatyard, Henry at the helm and me in charge of engine rotation and speed and when in the river a sense of responsibility slowly acquiring the feel of steering our portable home to our planned main port of call Great Yarmouth. Getting used to river traffic rules passing oncoming boats on our left and giving sailing craft a wide berth, extra care was given to yachts, especially when they were tacking downwind of us in the narrow river.

Our first day was used learning that manoeuvring our boat required a greater anticipation of movement ahead as its response to helm and engine power was much slower than driving a car, especially when coming alongside a prospective berth. A Broad near Wroxham provided our first anchorage, firstly giving us both ample practice of manoeuvring and get used to our new mode of life in a very small wooden house which was main bedroom come dining room, lounge, with galley attached on the after end and toilet for'd with third bunk, all within a space, in which one could not swing the proverbial 'cat'. At least the engine was located in the open cockpit fully exposed to the weather giving us a maritime experience of wind in the face, sun beating down on your head and on occasions rain pouring down one's neck, similar to cycling but with a 'luverly' little engine doing the pedalling, wonderful!

The extra money Henry and I had to provide, due to our absent pal, gave us the luxury of the main bunks and not to have drawn straws for the small bunk in the forepeak alongside the lavatory, which incidentally, flushed directly below water level into, broad, river or reed bed, wherever we had to 'pump the bilges'. I discovered this whilst swimming near the boat when Henry was simultaneously using the direct flushing system. This was an example of yesteryear practices that later caused over pollution by dramatic increase in population use, thereby making it essential for sewage to be contained and chemically treated.

We soon acquired skills in handling our vessel, keeping it shipshape, all fenders stowed neatly in the gunnels and not swinging untidily when underway. There was always some activity when sailing and to appreciate the picturesque view on our daily voyages. After leaving the more populated part of the broads at the low level at which we sailed with high banks made the sailing a little boring as one's view was limited to just miles of reeds.

I suppose as young men, scenery wasn't our main interest but the activities handling our ship, exploring lagoons, small lakes whose entrances were partly hidden by reed beds and the long voyage to Norwich and return, our main interest. On reaching Great Yarmouth we found that convenient berths required fees and any form of entertainment ashore made serious inroads to our limited finances, our stay was short. In addition the need to ensure we had sufficient cash for petrol and other bare essentials limited our cash flow for luxuries. Even the popular pink seaside rock, peppermint flavoured with the name right through the middle, was thought to be too big a drain on our finances.

After five days of adventure we approached Norwich, our planned outward-bound terminal port, but because of the industrial outlook on the riverbanks, decided not to progress further. This decision was enhanced because when we passed a Dutch coaster discharging alongside a quay, two young ladies on board waved and in the following banter, by our offer to entertain them on board, we promised to return after lunching downstream. At a suitable anchorage, half and hour down river, the galley was manned and the meal enjoyed on the cabin table with noticeable movement when a vessel passed. It was during the rice and sultana pudding session that we became aware that there was no movement the table was 'land locked'.

Our acquired sailing knowledge prompted us to go topside to investigate. To our consternation we found our ship firmly aground on black slimy mud exposed by an ebb tide. Fortunately, the stern was still water borne and so pleased we had a Quant (barge pole). Retrieving the bow anchor required some effort and to our concern pulled our boat further onto the smelly mud, but undaunted we pushed our trusty Quant firmly into at least two feet of the evil stuff, the boat moved inches towards free water, but when we, with great effort, retrieved the pole it pulled us back again to the starting point. Several attempts made us realise that a more dramatic method was needed to get afloat and keep our date with the girls. A crewmember must go over the side to back heave the bow off the clinging stuff. Coins were tossed and yours truly became the potential mud lark! I can still remember lowering myself into the black stuff eventually finding my descent stopped at thigh level. Ugh! What followed was a mud lark between me and the boat with shouts of encouragement from the lucky one above with promises to dowse me down with buckets of water when afloat. Luckily my efforts succeeded with the promised anointment after a swim and making sure my smelly body was clean and allowed on board. In retrospect I can't remember whether we tried with the engine astern to get us free but from my later knowledge at least it would have assisted my 'push of war'.

With great haste we washed the dishes because the unplanned mud anchorage had already delayed us way beyond our 'blind date' time and got underway with full speed ahead. From a distance, we viewed the coaster with eager anticipation but could see no waving females and when abeam the Dutchman, there were two well built foreign gentlemen giving us the 'weather eye'. We didn't bother to wave and altered course down stream. Whether the girls had given up waiting for us or the crew members on board were their parents who may have overhead that a couple of English men were returning to take them on a cruise, we shall never know. One often looks back over the years to similar incidents wondering if chance appointments missed, may have altered one's life course for the better or worse.

Our homeward voyage back to Wroxham via the same route was enjoyable and we were able to appreciate to a greater depth the features of the countryside around us because we were now experienced boat handlers. A certain element of monotony developed during the latter stages of our cruise as the 'mucking about in boats' became routine. We arrived back on the Saturday morning on time with the inventory complete and to the owner's satisfaction. I cannot remember if a deposit was made but I expect it was the custom because there must have been a high risk of loss or damage by 'first trippers'. Indeed I believe the size of boat we had was allocated on that basis, and we knew that should we return we would qualify for a larger vessel.

In retrospect, I had no inkling the Broads holiday seventy years ago proved to relate to my life's future course. Four years later, after I finished my apprenticeship, I joined the Merchant Navy as an Engineer Officer finding myself dealing with engines of 1,600/8,700 H.P. compared with King's 8 H.P. ECLIPSE, No. P 191 and was shipwrecked after only eight months at sea. Within another two years, lucky to survive four war years in various oceans of the world. My friendship with Henry and Stanley continued at T.M. Birketts, Henry became a senior metallurgist at Rolls Royce in Crewe and Stanley remained at Birketts becoming their Chief Chemist.

After my twelve years in the Merchant Navy I served the remainder of my professional life in power stations covering South East England from Norwich to Brighton and the Home Counties. My business travels introduced me to Norfolk and retirement in Diss, twenty-one years to date. The full circle association with Wroxham being completed last year when I became a member of the Norfolk Broads, Merchant Navy Association whose meetings are held at Sutton Staithe only a few miles from Wroxham seventy years after becoming Chief Engineer of No. P. 191.

At a recent M.N. Association meeting I was told the top left hand picture of a windmill at Horning was still there but was built as an imitation windmill. The building in the other picture at Potter Heigham, also still there, was originally a fairground helter-skelter with the furniture designed in the house to fit in the circular rooms and the top part in the garden as an outhouse. I was particularly interested to learn that the coal fired tug in the lower snap was most probably the United Services steam powered paddler towing a London sailing barge, sadly gone forever. However, one wonders whether it could be the one referred to in the E.D.P.'s newspaper cutting? Yare Steamboats (Sunday supplement 01-06-02) – reciprocating steam engines can last forever.

Yare steamboats

Taken from Norfolk and Norwich Notes and Queries
July 17, 1897

The first occasion that a steamboat appeared upon the river Yare was on August 10, 1813.

The vessel was described as a steam barge, and its passage from Yarmouth to Norwich was said to have "excited a considerable degree of curiosity, as numbers of people hastened to the river in various places to see it pass, and many awaited its arrival at the ferry".

It was a paddle steamer, and the descriptions given by the local newspapers were very quaint.

"Its principle of motion," it was stated, "is a number of oars something in the shape of a barn shovel. These are fixed in an axis forming a sort of water wheel, one on each side of the vessel, which are turned by machinery, which is put in motion by a small steam engine."

It was by no means a fast boat, five miles an hour was its top speed, and its punctuality was not always to be depended upon: "It seems likely to be a safe and convenient mode of conveyance to and from Yarmouth, and if the proprietor can get it to act in a manner so as to establish the certainty of its arrival, little doubt can be entertained but it will answer his purpose, as few people will regard the splashing of the oars or the noise of the machinery."

Another steamer, known as Wright's Norwich and Yarmouth steam-packet, was running in 1817. On Good Friday morning (April 4) it had just started from Foundry Bridge when its boiler burst, and killed five men and three children, besides wounding several others.

After that an ingenious person conceived the idea of propelling a boat with paddles worked by horse power, but nothing practical came of the suggestion. – J.A.H.

■ Any further information on these topics can be sent to Agricultural Editor Michael Pollitt at Prospect House, Norwich NR1 1RE or e-mail: michael.pollitt@archant.co.uk

CHAPTER FIFTEEN

AWAY TO SEA

After completing my apprenticeship I was disappointed that there was no increase in my wages to a journeyman's rate, three pounds ten shillings per week and sensing that T.M. Birkett's management showed no enthusiasm, in the foreseeable future, to increase my wages, I was prompted to explore other fields of employment.

Two representatives who regularly visited the firm, one from English Electric in Rugby and the other from British Petroleum, suggested I apply to their firms and they would make their recommendations. The E.E.C. representative thought the high-tension switchgear design department would be suitable with my qualifications and would speak to the Manager on my behalf. Mr MacLeod of B.P. was an ex. Chief Engineer from the Blue Star Line and thought I would be ideally suited for the mercantile marine. I knew of a number of Chief Engineers of firms in The Potteries, mining, steel works and silk mills who were all ex-marine engineers, and after listening to some of Mr. MacLeod's world travel stories his offer was given first priority.

I have no doubt that Mr MacLeod's telephone conversation with Mr. J. Douglas B.S.L. Chief Engineering Superintendent carried weight, because within a few weeks I was invited to join the 'Tacoma Star' at Hull. Such short notice made it impracticable for me to terminate my employment with T.M. Birkett and Sons. My letter of apology was answered with an instruction to report to B.S.L., St. Mary Axe, in a fortnight's time.

My appointment as an Assistant Engineer Officer with the Blue Star Line in London proved to be one of the most interesting periods of my life and somewhat dangerous during the war years. I served in ten steam and motor vessels and obtained the Ministry of Transport, First Class (Chief Engineer Steamship & Motorship) Certificate of Competency. My twelve years at sea are recorded in my book 'I SURVIVED'.

Since writing 'I SURVIVED' old shipmates have surfaced reminding me of many episodes, one of which may be of interest.

We left Victoria Docks in London on the s.s. ROYAL STAR shortly after October 18th 1941 joined an east coast (E-boat Alley) convoy in rough weather, complete with a barrage balloon attached to the stern. It was quite a sight watching the 'Balloon Man' with a number in tow delivering one to each ship with the obvious shout of 'How many jam jars do you want for it, mate'? often with unprintable replies.

The weather was blustery, visibility poor, when suddenly somewhere south of the Humber engine room emergency bells indicated trouble down below. Arriving on the engine room platform, one engine stopped, I think the port because heavy vibration with noisy clanking sounds aft indicated that something serious had happened to the propeller. The 'Bridge' thought we had sailed over a buoy or something obviously not a mine otherwise there would have been every need to stop the engine! Slowly moving the engine partly astern and ahead a few times seemed to have cleared whatever was fouling the propeller, but as engine revolutions increased, heavy vibration occurred with axial flutter on the multi-collared thrust. It was obvious we should leave the convoy to assess what damage had been sustained and repaired before proceeding with our voyage.

Hull was the nearest port, with a dry dock, which could provide facilities to inspect and hopefully repair damage found. The details of repair I cannot remember clearly but some blade damage was corrected to enable us to proceed after a few days in Hull.

Brief runs ashore between watches to relieve the sea-going tension were obviously taken up with vigour but wartime blackout etc. limited one's choice. However, I remember someone discovered that a small dance was available which we found was taking place in what I think was an old warehouse. Admission was six pence, which included a bottle of lemonade and entry up a flight of stairs. It was obviously a very local affair; probably run by a church society and we were met with curious stares from the young people seated on forms around the low ceiling room with a small band at the far end. I must admit that our civilian dress appeared a little 'up-market' when we began to take in our surroundings and when I asked where the cloakroom was situated, several fingers pointed to a rack above their heads along each side of the loft. We sensed by the immediate silence in our vicinity that we were 'out of our depth'. However, having placed our coats on the racks it was time for 'action stations' and to start the ball rolling. My first request to a lass "May I have this dance with you?" was shyly refused, but to my embarrassment I was turned down by the next three! It was my turn to sit down and lick my wounds. My companions also found that a barrier existed. It was time to 'size up' and observe how the natives performed.

It soon became apparent that the young men's approach to a girl for a dance was to say "Are you getting up?" at the same time yanking the girl into his manly embrace. We were successful from then on using the same technique and although not quite blending in with the locals we had a pleasant time before departing at half past nine to rejoin the old ROYAL.

Eventually, after leaving Hull in a 5-6 knot convoy around North Scotland we joined an Atlantic Convoy. Needless to say the vessel responsible for collecting the barrage balloons found many missing due to the high winds during our passage. Our voyage, after being released from a slow Atlantic Convoy, was unescorted to Cape Town, Port Elizabeth, East London and Durban delivering war materials. The remainder of that voyage is recorded in my book.

However, leaving South Africa we trundled our way to Australia loading food supplies and returned, unescorted, to Cape Town. It was the latter part of the voyage to Cape Town where a few anxious days occurred because our fuel oil became dangerously low. The passage across the Indian Ocean in cold adverse weather had contributed to our dilemma. The steam heating in the double-bottom tanks were minimal in old ships like the ROYAL STAR, only round the suction area therefore the cold seawater temperature retarded drainage of the heavy bunker oil. Speed was reduced to conserve fuel, with the fourth engineer continuously trying empty tanks and successfully pumping a few tons from them, which had drained over a period of time.   His efforts and those of other watch-keeping engineers were more than intensified in the effort to extract oil from the tanks, when plans had been discussed that any burnable material may have to be used including our cabin furniture, if the weather did not improve.   We arrived at Cape Town with great relief having only a few tons of fuel left in the working settling tank, and were quick to take on fuel as soon as the oil tender came alongside.

But we were to experience greater anxiety later on the final of our voyage when in a nine-knot convoy towing the senior RN escort a German submarine led the convoy.   Described in my book 'I SURVIVED'.

Ships of similar vintage to the ROYAL STAR no doubt contributed to the success of the Blue Star Line as well as the outcome of the war.   Sturdy no nonsense vessels, twin screws, reliable triple expansion steam engines, with coal-fired boilers, some later converted to oil, like the ROYAL STAR.   Never to be ocean greyhounds with sleek lines but slow, determined bull dogs, waddling around the world at a 'dogged' speed delivered their goods, frozen, homeward.

They also provided a sound training school for all crew members from Skipper through to deck boys, peggy's and 'spud barbers'.   The latter I well remember on the FRESCO STAR having to hand peel potatoes every day in all weathers, besides his other chores, enough for 70-80 men.

The FRESNO STAR was at Panama, homeward bound, when war was declared, which I have recorded in my book.

I well remember joining her as Fourth Engineer Officer in February 1939 prior to which I had sailed in larger, modern ships, STUART, AVELONA and AUSTRALIA STAR.   What a shock when I saw her on a dark rainy night listing against the quay at a North Shields Coaling Staithe.   With assistance from my taxi driver carrying suitcases over a plank gangway we scrambled over piles of coal on deck and finally finding my cabin by nameplate over the door.   Inside, everything I touched had a fine coating of coal dust, the small cabin lit by an electric light which was obviously being energised by a dynamo thumping away somewhere below the deck.   I was a little non-plussed, the taxi driver departed with a sympathetic grin, 'Nice little place you've got, good luck mate".

The following days were somewhat daunting, down below working on unfamiliar engines and in the stokehold with piles of coal and ash everywhere.   Knowing I would be in charge with the help of an assistant engineer, made me doubt whether marine engineering was 'my cup of tea'.   Fortunately, my coal firing experience on the STUART STAR gave me confidence knowing my challenge would be in the engine room.

Like many things in life, after getting over the first shock I soon settled down, one had to blend in with, what was to me, more basic conditions of shipboard life. Not surprisingly the months that followed made me realise what a happy tough hard working time it proved to be.   Indeed in retrospect, I consider that my time on the STUART, FRESNO and ROYAL STAR had a lasting effect on my sea-going days and the experience a benefit later during my working life.

SKETCH OF MY CABIN
ON THE s.s. ROYAL STAR
18.10.41 – 27.5.42

1. Compactum
2. Bulkhead Dynamo

THE OLD BATTLE SQUADRON

In the Blue Star Line, THE OLD BATTLE SQUADRON, was the term given to the smaller old ships, built before or during the 1914-18 war; ALBION STAR, FRESNO STAR, CELTIC STAR, GAELIC STAR, NORMAN STAR, ROYAL STAR and TACOMA STAR.

The CELTIC, ROYAL and TACOMA were lost during the Second World War but the remainder survived.

I think one should salute the ships of THE OLD BATTLE SQUADRON and the men who sailed in them, particularly the senior officers and men who spent many years on them; they were their homes. Indeed they played a major part in keeping the vessels maintained and seaworthy both deck and engine room departments contributed. The skippers and chief engineers knew their ships' idiosyncrasies, the captains knowing how to sail their creaking old hulls and the Chief Engineers understanding how to keep their hearts beating soundly in the worlds weather zones.

This intimate knowledge of the working machinery down below was ably illustrated by my chief, Mr. Alex Brown, on the FRESNO STAR. As fourth engineer, in addition to my routine visit to his cabin after noon with the logbook, it was repeated after midnight, to report that all was well below. It was his way of making me appreciate that I was keeping his watch (8 to 12) for him. Generally, it was a cursory reply from his bunk, "Thank you Mr. Swain, good night" to my "Everything OK Chief". On some occasions however, he would ask why certain auxiliaries had been changed over, illustrating how the engine room sounds gave him a clear picture of what was happening down below. Sound was often the first sense in the cacophony of noise to indicate that something abnormal was happening in the compact machinery space with smell and sight following.

My routine visit to Mr. Brown was repeated on one unforgettable night, September 3rd 1939 (recorded in my book), when after my usual call, I tuned in my wireless to hear that the ATHENIA had been torpedoed. My agitated return visit with the news was met with an offhand retort 'So the blooming fun has started!'

There must have been many incidents during the sea going years of THE OLD BATTLE SQUADRON true events that perhaps have never been recorded; an example may have been when the FRESNO STAR was damaged while negotiating the narrow passage (Kirke Narrow), to Puerto Natales from the Straits of Magellan. It was before my time on the FRESNO and the story was of her damaging her stern during the latter part of her passage and being caught in a strong adverse riptide 8-9 knots. She managed, with both watertight doors shut, to enter the port with the stern space and propeller tunnels flooded. The passage through was always critical for the slower vessels, as they had to wait in daylight for high water, having only about half an hour to get through. I was told that a small boat used to monitor the state of the tide and signalled to the pilot when slack water occurred, so that the waiting ship(s) made full steam ahead move.

Dangerous currents at high tide from deck of M.V. PEURTO EDEN
When passing through the notorious Paso Kirke

Puerto Montt – Peurto Natales, Patagonia, Chile
February 1997
My thanks to Mr Alan Durand: pictures taken en route

Mr Middleditch who was the Fourth Engineer with me on the STUART left to join the GAELIC STAR as Third and told me recently that his voyage was also to Puerto Natales and he remembers seeing the FRESNO STAR on the other side of the sea loch. He also vividly remembers their passage through the 'bottleneck' when all officers were on standby and he was on duty in the steering gear flat to ensure that the engine functioned correctly. The width of the passage, to him, only seemed twice the beam of the ship and an additional hazard at one end was a submerged reef, which was marked from one side by a fixed horizontal pole. He recalls the port was a remote settlement, only a few houses, the Frigorifico being the largest to which, he was told, the sheep were herded hundreds of miles from the surrounding, inhospitable countryside. A community hall served for limited entertainment, which during his visit a cinema show was arranged. He recalls the inhabitants explained that they had to switch off all unnecessary lights and heating so that the small diesel power station could provide the extra current for the cinema projectors.

The main source of damage to the FRESNO was that many rivets had been ripped out and all efforts to pump out the stern failed because of the limited bilge suction points. Presumably, in those days, no assistance was available from the shore authorities with additional pumps in order to raise the stern off the bottom to expose the damaged area to carry out repairs. A critical decision was made by Mr Brown with assistance from the Chief Refrigerating Engineer (whose name I can't remember) to progressively open the watertight doors using both main circulating pumps on bilge injection. The much larger pumping capacity of these pumps was able to overcome the leakage flow into the engine room, thus enabling access to the damaged area. Rivet holes were sealed temporarily with wooden plugs and presumably the ship trimmed down by the head to expose the damaged area. Repairs were made which enabled the FRESNO to continue on her voyage.

A commendable example of innovative duties by senior officers which was common practice in days of yore, before ports in remote corners of the globe acquired repair facilities and air freight able to transport equipment and spares at short notice.

40. FRESNO STAR (I) (1929 — 1947)
ON. 141930. 7998g, 5020n. 449.5 × 58.2 × 37.1 feet.
Two T.3-cyl. by the shipbuilder, driving twin screws.
12.7.1919: Launched by Barclay, Curle and Co. Ltd., Glasgow, (Yard No. 572), as WOODARRA for British India Steam Navigation Co. Ltd., London. (She had been laid down as WAR APOLLO for The Shipping Controller). *11.1919:* Completed. *8.1929:* Purchased by Blue Star Line (1920) Ltd. and renamed FRESNO STAR. *1930:* Owners restyled as Blue Star Line Ltd. *1933:* Transferred to Union Cold Storage Co. Ltd. (Blue Star Line Ltd. managers). *1935:* Transferred to Frederick Leyland and Co. Ltd. — same managers. *1947:* Sold to British Iron and Steel Corporation for demolition, allocated to T. W. Ward Ltd. and work commenced *7.1947* at Inverkeithing, Scotland.

FRESNO STAR   *Tom Rayner*

ROYAL STAR   *J. Clarkson*

19. ROYALSTAR/ROYAL STAR (I) (1919 — 1944)
ON. 142772. 7900g, 4880n. 450.0 × 58.5 × 37.1 feet.
Two T.3-cyl. by the shipbuilder, driving twin screws.
22.11.1918: Launched by Workman, Clark and Co. Ltd., Belfast, (Yard No. 438), as WAR CHARON for The Shipping Controller, and completed *2.1919* as ROYALSTAR for Royalstar S.S. Co. Ltd. (The Blue Star Line Ltd., managers). *1920:* Transferred to Union Cold Storage Co. Ltd. (Blue Star Line (1920) Ltd., managers). *1929:* Renamed ROYAL STAR. *1930:* Managers restyled as Blue Star Line Ltd. *11.3.1941:* Bombed and gunned by enemy aircraft while lying off Stonehaven, Scotland. *20.4.1944:* Torpedoed and sunk by aircraft, N.E. of Algiers, Algeria in position 37.02N, 03.41E, while on a voyage from Buenos Aires, Argentine Republic and Algiers to Malta, Taranto, Italy, and Alexandria, Egypt with 5,300 tons of refrigerated and 350 tons of dehydrated meats. One crew member was lost.

Ship details courtesy - The Blue Star Line.

NORMAN STAR   F. W. Hawks

20.   ALMEDA (I)/NORMANSTAR/NORMAN STAR (I) (1919 — 1950)
ON. 143398. 6817g, 4340n. 415.6 × 56.2 × 25.5 feet.
T.3-cyl. by the shipbuilder.
19.4.1919: Launched by Dunlop, Bremner and Co. Ltd., Port Glasgow, (Yard No. 290), as ALMEDA
for Almeda S.S. Co. Ltd. (The Blue Star Line Ltd. managers), and completed *10.1919* as

NORMAN STAR in war-time   W.S.P.L.

TACOMA STAR   J. Clarkson

39.   TACOMA STAR (I) 1929 — 1942)
ON. 141910. 7924g, 4704n. 450.0 × 58.5 × 37.1 feet.
Two T.3-cyl. by the shipbuilder.
30.4.1919: Launched by Workman, Clark and Co. Ltd., Belfast, (Yard No. 440), as WANGARATTA
for British India Steam Navigation Co. Ltd., London. (She had been laid down as WAR THESEUS
for The Shipping Controller). *4.1929:* Purchased for £63 000 by Blue Star Line (1920) Ltd. and
renamed TACOMA STAR. *1930:* Owners restyled as Blue Star Line Ltd. *1933:* Transferred to Union
Cold Storage Co. Ltd. (Blue Star Line Ltd., managers). *1935:* Transferred to Frederick Leyland and
Co. Ltd. — same managers. *3.5.1941:* Struck by a high explosive bomb and settled on the dock
bottom at Liverpool. *7/8.5.1941:* Struck by incendiary bombs and further damaged, but *1.6.1941*
raised and dry-docked and repaired. *1.2.1942:* Torpedoed and sunk by the German submarine
U.109, 38 miles E. of Hampton Roads, U.S.A. in a position 37.33N, 69.21W. She was on a voyage
from Buenos Aires, Argentine Republic and Hampton Roads, U.S.A. to the United Kingdom with
5,107 tons of general cargo. Her crew of 85 was lost.

GAELIC STAR   F. W. Hawks

16.   MONTILLA/GAELICSTAR/GAELIC STAR (1917 — 1949)
ON. 140302. 5595g, 3528n. 389.8 × 53.2 × 24.7 feet.
T.3-cyl. by D. Rowan and Co., Glasgow.
22.2.1917: Launched by Russell and Co., Port Glasgow, (Yard No. 693), as MONTILLA for Montilla
S.S. Co. Ltd. (The Blue Star Line Ltd. managers). *8.1917:* Completed. *1920:* Transferred to Union
Cold Storage Co. Ltd. (Blue Star Line (1920) Ltd. managers), and renamed GAELICSTAR. *1929:*
Renamed GAELIC STAR. *1930:* Managers restyled as Blue Star Line Ltd. *8.1949:* Sold to
Compagnia Genovese di Navigazione a Vapore S.A., Italy, for £30,000 and renamed CAPO NOLI.
1950: Sold to Gestioni Esercizio Navi — G.E.N., Italy. *1956:* Transferred to Gestioni Esercizio Navi
— Sicilia G.E.N.S. Italy. *1959:* Sold to Sidemar for demolition, and work commenced *1.7.1959* at
Trieste, Italy.

90

CELTIC STAR

Brownell collection

18. CAMANA/CELTICSTAR/CELTIC STAR (I) (1917 — 1943)
ON. 142437. 5574g, 3466n. 390.7 × 53.2 × 24.7 feet.
T.3-cyl. by the shipbuilder.
3.12.1917: Launched by Dunlop, Bremner and Co. Ltd., Port Glasgow, (Yard No. 289) as CAMANA
for Camana S.S. Co. Ltd. (The Blue Star Line Ltd., managers). *6.1918:* Completed. *1920:*
Transferred to Union Cold Storage Co. Ltd. (Blue Star Line (1920) Ltd., managers), and renamed
CELTICSTAR. *1929:* Renamed CELTIC STAR. *1930:* Managers restyled as Blue Star Line Ltd.
1935: Following the lengthening of AVELONA STAR 12,858/27, this vessel's funnel was fitted
to CELTIC STAR. *30.3.1943:* Torpedoed and sunk by the Italian submarine FINZI, S.W. of
Freetown, Sierra Leone in position 04.16N, 17.44W, whilst on a voyage from Manchester,
Greenock and Freetown to Montevideo, Uruguay and Buenos Aires, Argentine with 4,410 tons
of general cargo, including mail. Two crew members were lost.

CELTIC STAR, post-1935 appearance

ALBION STAR

J. Clarkson

21. ALBIONSTAR/ALBION STAR (I) (1919 — 1948)
ON. 143286. 7920g, 4908n. 450.0 × 58.5 × 37.1 feet.
Two T.3-cyl. by the shipbuilder, driving twin screws.
6.3.1919: Launched by Workman, Clark and Co. Ltd., Belfast, (Yard No. 439), as WAR HECUBA
for The Shipping Controller (Commonwealth and Dominion Line Ltd. managers), and completed
6.1919 as ALBIONSTAR for Albionstar S.S. Co. Ltd. (The Blue Star Line Ltd. managers). *1920:*
Transferred to Union Cold Storage Co. Ltd. (Blue Star Line (1920) Ltd. managers). *1929:* Renamed
ALBION STAR. *1930:* Managers restyled as Blue Star Line Ltd. *1948:* Sold to British Iron and
Steel Corporation, allocated to T. W. Ward Ltd. and *23.4.1948* arrived at Briton Ferry to be broken
up.

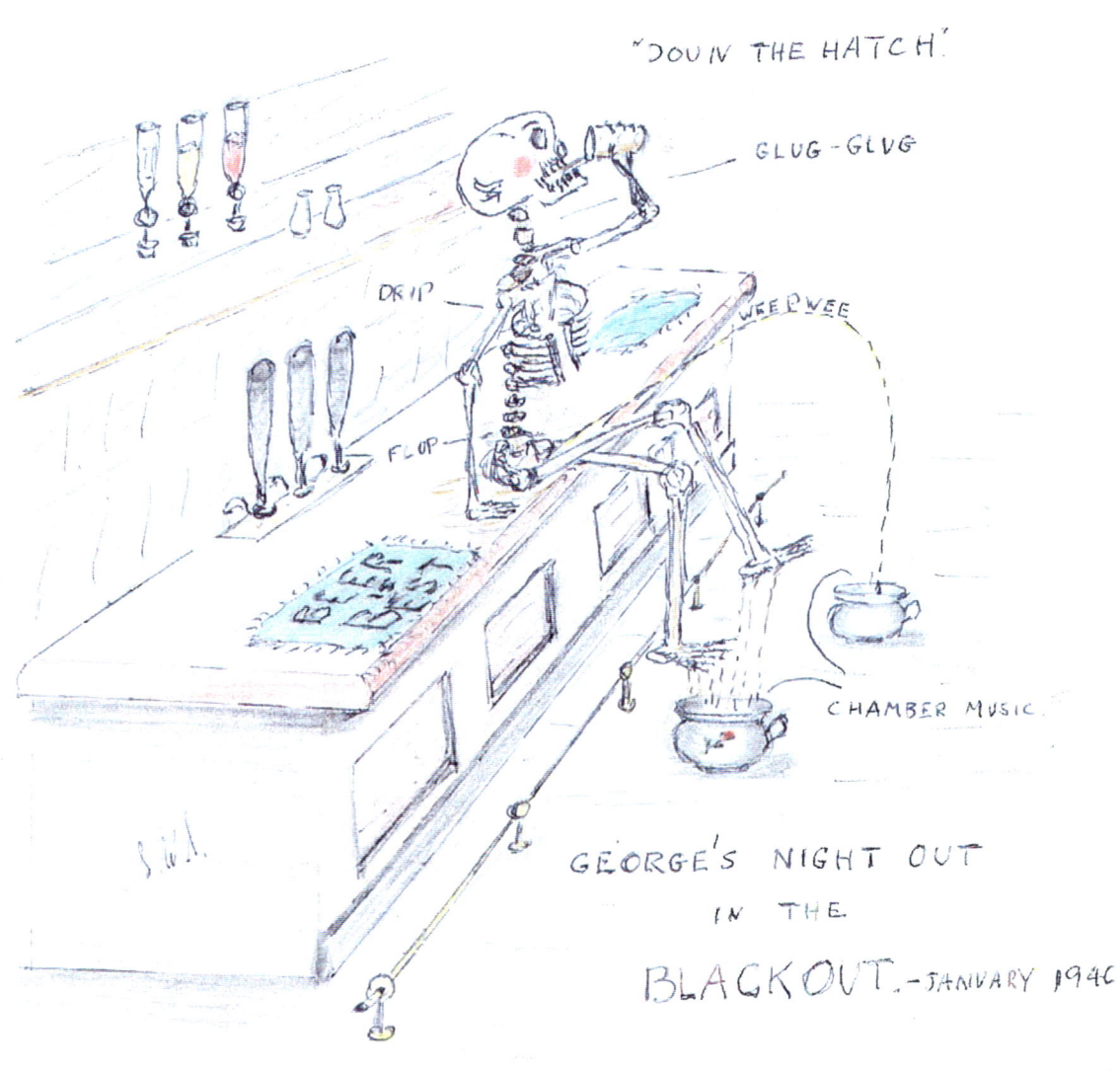

"DOWN THE HATCH"

GLUG - GLUG

DRIP

WEE WEE

FLOP

CHAMBER MUSIC

GEORGE'S NIGHT OUT
IN THE
BLACKOUT. - JANUARY 1940

FEBRUARY 2001

MEDICAL TREATMENT – MERCHANT NAVY STYLE

I suppose, because of the absence of a doctor on merchant ships, except passenger or if a ship was carrying over a hundred crewmembers a sensible, albeit sometimes rough, medical knowledge and treatment was necessary in the Merchant Navy. The Second Mate, in the Blue Star Line, was usually responsible for any medical treatment and indeed first aid and lifeboat certificates were necessary before a deck officer would sit for his 'ticket'. (Certificate of Competency).

It was during my wartime stay at the British Sailors Society's head office, on the corner of East and West India Dock Road, studying for my Chief's Ticket when a couple of deck officers took one of their learning aids for an outing. They decided to take 'George' a skeleton for a night out to Aldgate one Saturday night. 'George' was a complete, fully wire-connected skeleton, which hung in the classroom and was used for first aid lessons. The fun started when, in the blackout, they boarded a bus, sitting in the fore and aft seats at the rear with George sitting on their knees between them asking for tickets to Aldgate, half price for him because he wasn't taking a seat. Typical of the London conductor, never short of quips, responded "Has he lost his ration book?" The looks on some of the passengers faces cannot be described here also the flow of remarks when they took George into a pub for a drink. Suffice to say that the pints donated to him to build him up, were downed by them, apologising because he couldn't hold his liquor! The return journey was even more hilarious as everyone was in a very happy mood, except George whose bottom jaw came off having been overworked during many ventriloquist acts. It was repaired and he was hung up to bed after a very memorable night out.

However, I was to become the patient for the Second Mate during one of my wartime voyage.

OPERATION – FINGER

While anchored awaiting a berth on the EMPIRE MIGHT at Littleton, Christchurch, New Zealand our final loading port, one of my colleagues was line fishing; asked me to take over while he made a call to the 'heads'. He instructed me on how to sense by feel on the line if it became engaged and to make another cast when it drifted too far with the current. Retrieving the line for a cast, I enthusiastically swung it round like a bolas allowing the weighted line to slip through my fingers. It suddenly stopped in flight by a hook impaling in my finger. Being a non-fishing type I did not realise that there were more above the two hooks near the weight. The heavy gauge hook had buried itself in my finger with the barb out of sight. I was detached from the line by Mr Davidson, the Second Engineer, and complete with hook and the Second Mate who was O/C first aid went to the small hospital accommodation.

My case was examined carefully and the Second Mate was preparing lance etc., to cut out the hook when fortunately for me Mr Davidson thought the hook could be removed by cutting off the eye and then pushing the remainder through my finger, estimating it would miss the bone on the way through and save stitching etc. It was decided that this option should be tried first, pushing the hook through making a circular tour round the bone. The second returned with a pair of pliers with cutting facility and we all took a tot of local anaesthetic an amber coloured liquid from bonny Scotland.

I was then seated in a chair with Mr Davidson sitting on me with my arm through his legs, the idea being that it would keep me firmly in place and unable to see the operation. The eye of the hook was cut off and I was allowed to see the first stage of my operation and a second tot of medicinal comfort downed. We then resumed our operating positions with the second mate holding my finger firmly on a table. The pushing then started and after two movements I was informed the barb was in sight; seconds later the hook was pulled out so neatly that its entry and exit had to be pointed out to me and it was difficult getting iodine into the holes. A celebratory tot of medicinal comfort was taken all round on a very successful operation with a sigh of relief from me and the Second Mate because he had not been keen to use the scalpel anyway.

s.s. SAMTAY
OPERATION – FOOT

Another medical emergency developed whilst serving on the SAMTAY (1946) at an Indonesian port when a bare footed stevedore cut the sole of his foot on a deck fitting. The man was not concerned with his wound but the Mate did not appreciate footprints of blood over the deck, so he asked the Second Mate to stitch the fellow up. When the 'Doctor' attempted to put stitches in the two inch cut he could not push the needle through the tough eight-inch skin. A call for assistance to the engineering department resulted in me inspecting the job. My first suggestion of using a red-hot needle because we did not have a watchmaker's drills was ruled out as we thought the smell would upset the patient. It was decided I would return with breast drill and small gauge drill, suitably dressed in a clean white boiler suit wearing a white cap cover thereby presenting a clinical appearance.

The usual tots of medicinal comfort were to hand for the patient and operating staff, when by gesticulation we discovered he was a Muslim, so we shared his tot; it was easier than returning it to the bottle. I sterilised the small drill with a match flame, which was suitably marked so that I would not over drill. Our patient was placed on his stomach with leg raised and foot in position like a cobbler's last and my first drilling proved easier than expected and stopped as soon as I saw blood, the patient obviously feeling no pain. More holes were drilled and the cut clewed up when the Second Mate put in place suitable 'homeward bound' stitches.

A successful operation was celebrated in the usual manner and our patient given a sitting down job driving a steam winch.

Among many 'rude awakenings' I experienced during my first and early voyages was when a colleague acquired an infestation of pubic body lice, affectionately known as a dose of CRABS! The usual treatment was the removal of the pubic hairs, the region covered with mercurial ointment and a toilet allocated for the patient's private use. To protect his clothes he would use old underpants aft to for'd for a few days until such time as the lice had disappeared with the pants 'over the side'. The problem caused more amusement than worry and it was generally known that lavatory seats were not really to blame. The patient soon had to come clean when it was suggested that lavatory seats were not usually called Lolita, Cleopatra or Anita.

There was never a shortage of mercurial ointment because usually one or two hundred weight drums were kept in the propeller shaft tunnel. It was carried in the event of a propeller being removed or replaced and was used to coat the tapered tail end shaft before it was refitted to prevent it seizing on the shaft. I now knew why it was called 'crab fat'.

On one of my voyages I suffered a continuous attack of boils and visited my doctor, Dr. Hallam, whose surgery was in Waterloo Road, Burslem, for treatment whilst on leave. He told me that he would like a sample of puss from an active boil from which a vaccine could be made, explaining that it was the best treatment. Needless to say, when I visited him after the next two-month voyage only one small boil was available and was not active enough for his proposed treatment and it transpired to be the end of my problem.

During my visit I asked him what was the medical name for Crabs because I thought it would be interesting to know the correct name. At first he hadn't a clue what I was talking about, presumably Staffordshire only had a small population of seafarers bringing back exotic medical problems with simple names. After further information he removed a large medical book from a shelf and eventually showed a page giving pictures of nine different species of body lice. "Which one was it?" he asked. I was unable to answer I had never seen a magnification of the little blighters as the pictures showed.

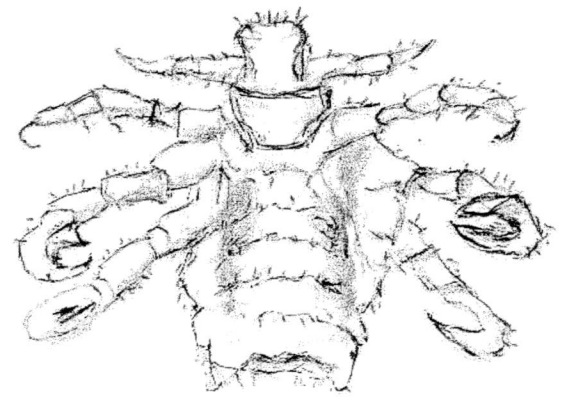

Crab Louse
PTHIRUS PUBIS
About 40 Times Life Size

Indeed even then to me the differences were small, the main feature being they all had many legs. I departed agreeing with the doctor that crabs was the best word because it covered the whole species. He also explained that the female burrowed under the skin to lay her eggs, which incubated three or four days later thereby releasing another invasion. He added that he did not think it necessary to shave away the 'forest', which provided their habitat, but it was essential that continuing to apply the mercurial fodder to catch the second generation.

Some years later, as a Senior Officer, (Father figure) and from the doctor's advice I was able to provide and recommend treatment to a young officer who had been invaded under the sign of Cancer. He approached me saying that he was worried that he seemed to have what he thought was sawdust in the pubic region, which he was unable to remove by washing. On examination in my cabin and removal of one of the bits of sawdust, holding it up to the light, I was able to show him that it was a wee creature very much alive and kicking seen by the many legs in action. Naturally he was very worried but I was able to reassure him that it was a simple problem provided he followed the treatment already described. A separate toilet was allocated and his morale boosted by his fellow officers during frequent visits to his cabin and enquiring how his 'company' was keeping and how lucky he was that for a few days he would never be lonely. After ten or twelve days his foully area was clear of the 'dust' and the occasion celebrated in the usual manner.

Picture of engine room staff off duty
s.s. BRASIL STAR August 6th 1948 (three officers on watch)
Left-Right: Mr Alexander-Assistant Eng. Mr Walsham-Chief Refrig.
SWS-Second Eng. (Dr. Saw-rings) Mr Fraser-Second Elec.
Dr. Gibbons (Dr. Saw-bones) Mr Waugh-Senior Third Eng.
Mr MacGarry-Second Refrig. Mr White-Fourth Eng.
Mr Henson-Assistant Eng. Mr Pearcy-Chief Elec.
Mr Hocking-Assistant Eng. And Mr Ward-Chief Eng.

s.s. BRASIL STAR – 1947
Operations – Gold Rings and Crabs

I was personally involved in medical action on one or two occasions during my last years at sea whilst Second Engineer Officer on the BRASIL STAR. I acted as 'surgeon' by very carefully sawing off ladies golden rings on infected swollen fingers. The important pre-operation need being to smear the vicinity of the ring with Vaseline so that the gold dust from my metal saw was captured and carefully spirited into a receptacle to be recovered later. I might add no bloodletting occurred during the operation and the split ring carefully opened and removed with great relief from the female patient. Looking back over the years I think a drink provided by the relieved lady passengers was a reasonable fee for my professional services! Apparently when our doctor suggested the ring should be removed he explained that in sea-going parlance he was known as 'Doctor Saw-bones' and he would call on 'Doctor Saw-rings' to operate on his patient.

Professional engineers knew that preventative maintenance on plant or machinery reduces potential break down. Similarly in other walks of life the same principle applies especially in the medical field, prevention is better than cure.

I was fortunate because my father, before I started my working career, advised me that should I have personal health problems, I must always consult him first or the doctor. He explained that often when work mates were confided in, their knowledge was inferior and dangerous, so delay in medical attention could have serious consequences. He made it very clear I was beginning an adult life, where venereal and other contagious diseases were prevalent; I was also fortunate that as a teenager I saw a film on V.D. mentioned in 'A PALACE OF VARIETY'.

The Merchant Service also provided, by Senior Officers and men, information to guard young men particularly 'First Trippers' on where to go and places to avoid and also to be well aware of physical and medical dangers lurking ashore. It will always be imprinted in my mind that when I was leaving the STUART STAR on my first trip ashore in Buenos Aires that Mr Roberts the Second Engineer, to whom I was Watch Keeping Assistant, said "Have you got your Mackintosh?" (condom) to which I replied "It looks a beautiful evening, so sign of rain". He replied "You will know

97

how a weather front in the meteorological sense can make a dramatic change to our well-being?" I nodded. "Well out there in the largest metropolis in the southern hemisphere there are hundreds of female fronts who could dramatically change your senses, especially after you have had a drink, so be prepared, I've seen too many young men discovering they had inherited a 'hot rod' after a few days homeward bound, giving we Senior Officers concern. Not only for their well-being but also maintaining a full Watch Keeping force, so that we arrive on the scheduled day and tide in the Thames".

BUENOS AIRES

To the reader unfamiliar with the aforementioned term, the following may help. On steam reciprocating engines the piston rod, which travels in and out of the cylinder, is sealed with a gland, which can malfunction causing the gleaming steel rod to overheat thereby requiring the engine's speed to be reduced with adjustment and special treatment to cure what could be serious marine engineering problems.

Some years ago I read THE OXFORD BOOK OF EXPLORATION by Robin Hanbury-Tenison and was interested to learn that seafarers problems never change.

In the chapter SAMUEL WALLIS (1728-1795) and account by John Hawksworth, describes the discovery of Tahiti (1767). The ladies ashore demanded nails for their favours (a short time for a long nail) and because iron nails among other trinkets were used to barter they were carefully guarded. Consequently, nails from the ship's hull particularly from the cleats on the main deck, were purloined by some members of the crew, seriously endangering the ship's sea worthiness!

At least we never had to inspect the hull for missing rivets on our ships but the dangers ashore for we innocent seafarers were always there. Thank goodness some things never change!

Many well-known expressions of today originated from the days of sailing ships with the meaning of some applicable and used today. 'Show a leg' for example was the call of the Bosun or Petty Officer when calling the next watch for duty. It gave the ladies a modicum of privacy in the hammocks or bunks by showing a leg so their hairy companions were tufted out for duty and they were left to slumber on.

'Son of a Gun' a term given to a young boy or man with a sea faring heritage, I believe, was derived from the suggestion his mother conceived against or over the barrel of a gun, the gun deck being the only place where a degree of privacy was available, away from the crowded decks below. Another version was when a mother was having difficulty giving birth and was placed near a gun, which was fired, the noise and shock supposedly helping the lady with her difficulty!

PRESERVING THE ENVIRONMENT

It would seem that we M.N. types were already much aware of the importance of recycling waste products.

On the long storm bound voyages homeward bound on the SYDNEY STAR, a favourite pastime was to play cards, the stakes being cigarettes, which by their constant use lost tobacco before the half filled ones were scrapped. The card games in a small cabin after dinner were fully occupied by six to eight officers and ventilation limited to keep warm. The inevitable need to break wind after a food meal occurred and the game rudely halted with the cry 'lights out', when the crier cocked his stern, produced a fart, which was ignited in the confined, darkened cabin. A Marine Engineer's practical solution to remove obnoxious smells at source, providing clean air and at the same time producing a musical Aurora Borealis or Australis, depending in which hemisphere we were sailing. After the event an examination of the individual's pants for signs of singeing thus ensuring his 'foo foo' valve was working properly!

On the subject of methane, we marine engineers were always aware of its potential energy use. During my apprenticeship, I was often required (outside of normal working hours) to assist with the maintenance of a small National oil engine, which provided 110 volt D.C. electricity for Hawkstone Park Hotel and Golf Course, Shropshire (owned by a director of T.M. Birkett & Sons). In the stables area, where the engine room with the large glass storage batteries above was situated, well away from the hotel was the sewerage plant.

I well remember the time when consideration was given to converting the oil engine to use methane from the adjacent sewage plant; dramatically reducing it's operating cost. In such an installation the exhaust pipe from the engine would be altered to run through the 'sludge beds' to increase the release of gas and being advised that it would be one of my main duties if the change was made. One can imagine how relieved I was when it was estimated that there was insufficient gas for the project, especially when it may have needed the hotel chef to arrange 'special meals' to provide extra gas during peak periods for electricity!

CHAPTER SIXTEEN

NOTTINGHAM

Nottingham became a familiar city to me, being only twenty miles from Newark, and frequently visited during my childhood years with Grandma Swain. Also, during the war on leave from the Merchant Navy and my first shore job at Staythorpe Power Station, a village near Newark.

It was an interesting city claiming to be a gem of the Midlands having many beautiful, old and new buildings but I remember after the war, the book 'No Mean City' a story about Glasgow being the most notorious city with crime etc., it was said that Nottingham was not far behind.

However, it was where my mother met father in a theatre queue outside the Theatre Royal, lucky me. She was with a friend, a local girl who managed a café, but mother was from the great metropolis – London. Mother, after early years in 'service' worked for Boots the Chemist in their picture-framing department in London. Whether she volunteered or was asked to work in the Nottingham factory I have no knowledge but she must have been adventurous for those times because I suspect in the days of 1912 there were not many young women working away from home.

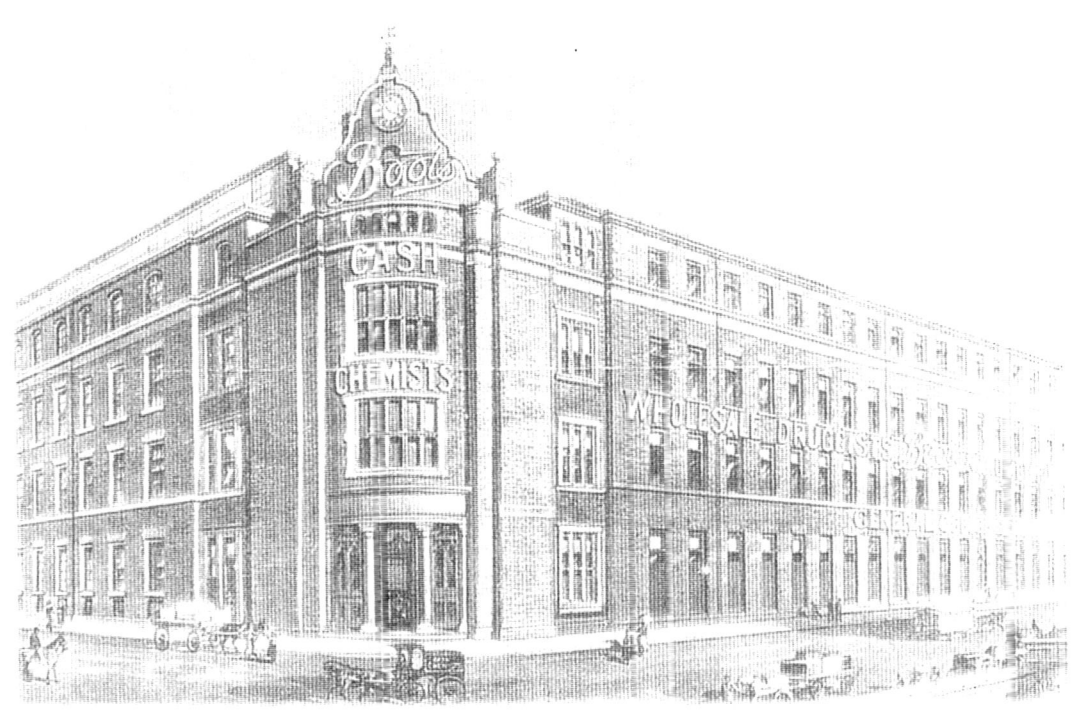

HEAD OFFICES OF BOOTS PURE DRUG COMPANY LTD
STATION STREET, NOTTINGHAM

I was always intrigued why Boots should be making picture frames and unfortunately never asked mother what particular job she did. Recently I enquired about the history of The Boots Company who have kindly sent me their history pack with a picture of where, I think, my mother worked.

On enquiry, Anita Logue, of The Boots Company Archives forwarded me the following report:

"Boots were involved in picture framing for a long period (1890-1986) and its introduction owes much to Jesse Boot's wife, Florence, who extended the appeal of the chemist stores by introducing gift, art and stationery departments, cafes and book lover's libraries".

My father had served a six-year apprenticeship as a cordwainer in Newark. I have no idea how long their courtship lasted but when he acquired a foreman's position with the Burslem Co-Operative Society in Stoke-on-Trent, they married, starting their life together in rented accommodation in Wolstanton, Newcastle-under-Lyme, Staffordshire.

During the war, I often visited Nottingham when on leave and enjoyed shows at the Theatre Royal, and most likely waited in a similar queue to my parents some fifty years later.

MOTHER & FATHER'S
WEDDING – 04.08.1913

FATHER - TEENAGER

CHAPTER SEVENTEEN

EPILOGUE

In the chapter, 'GOING TO SEA', I referred to my book 'I SURVIVED' which was published in November 1994, recording some of the highlights of my twelve years at sea, 1937-49. I derived a great pleasure from the many letters I received from readers, including shipmates with whom I had sailed instigating very nostalgic reunions.

It's sale was wide spread, copies dispatched to South Africa, Australia, New Zealand, USA, Sweden, Canada, France, Ljublijana, even the Isle of Man. Confirming Merchant Navy men originate from or settle all over the world. A great benefit, I think, to one's appraisal of other countries' cultures.

Letters of appreciation are usually uplifting but I did receive one from an eighty six year old lady, which was quite upsetting. Her nephew (a seventy year old MN Engineer Officer) read the book and with some apprehension decided to give it to her because her first husband, boy and girl sweethearts, was lost during the war on a Blue Star Ship. Her first and only child was born in 1943 and he never saw his daughter. As my career followed a similar pattern to her lost husband (some years my senior), she wanted another copy for her fifty-one year old daughter. One small consolation, the Skipper was among the survivors and he told her that the cable of the birth had been received and the baby's head was 'wet' in true Merchant Navy style. I resorted to phoning her, it was my only way of answering her request because I was emotionally moved. I found she was wheelchair bound but cheerful and 'bright as a button' like her letter.

Little has been written about the steadfast women behind their men, there must be hundreds who suffered similarly and relatives who would like to hear, in this case, from shipmates who knew their next of kin. There is no doubt today a great interest exists by the 40-70 year olds about the war years, many wishing to know more about the men and women involved, especially their relatives.

My early years at sea gave me the advantage of seeing many places, albeit mostly ports and to my mind have now become westernised and lost much of their cultural appearance and way of life.

It was only from my early voyages and throughout my sea-going time that I appreciated the important role that The Potteries played in supplying the world with high class crockery and sanitary ware. All the main street 'posh' shops (port out – starboard home) in the major ports displayed Staffordshire pots and some of the out of the way places. I never ceased to silently applaud the designers and workforce of the many 'Potbanks' whose wares were purchased with pride. Calls of nature, in my case, always stimulated an interest where the sanitary ware was made. Many times my colleagues would nod with disdain until I explained that I was only looking to see whose trademark was on the urinal.

Another important feature of my early voyages was when shipmates asked questions about Arnold Bennett, (the author), when they knew I came from Burslem, and my embarrassment at being unable to answer. My interest in things engineering had channelled me away from literary subjects, but this was dramatically corrected on later voyages by reading some of his books. I was then able to claim a close connection with A.B. when I discovered my first two years at night school were spent in the Wedgwood Institute – his day school. To emphasise the distinction of being born a 'Boslemite' would quote "So they thinks they kost but cona. Wot? Kickabo aginst awo unbostit. (So you think you can but you can't. What? Kick a ball against a wall and burst it). My Amstrad spell check was out of its depth on the foregoing sentence.

From then on I was able to claim that I knew at least one foreign language.

Not quite MADAME TUSSAUD's but it's a beginning! The local Museum Curator in Diss put on an exhibition to commemorate the end of War II and used my old reefer jacket with three prints to represent the Merchant Navy. One is a fine sketch, very similar to ATLANTIC AHEAD, by a crew member of R.M. s.s. QUEEN ELIZABETH 1942 of a convoy with a Liberty Ship in the lead and Flower Class Corvette escort. It was sent to me by Captain Brian Hope, the Chairman of Project Liberty Ship, Baltimore, with s.s. JOHN W. BROWN literature, in response to him receiving a copy of "I SURVIVED" for their library. The second picture of the EMPIRE MIGHT, page 57 in my book, which the Curator thought was a good example of a round the world wartime ship's maiden voyage and the third a photocopy of the relevant page in my discharge book.

1. BEFORE

2. ACTION STATIONS

3. AFTER

My first sight of the dummy (picture 1) looked more like a ruddy U-boat Commander that a MN Officer, no shirt or tie. The following week I proceeded to put matters right (pictures 2) with white shirt and black tie, the only one I have, (I worried that I may have required it before the exhibition ended, attending funerals become more frequent in my age bracket!). I had just completed the re-dress of the dummy when a father with a six-foot teenage son asked what V.G. stood for in the discharge book entry. I informed him that it meant 'very good conduct' he laughed and replied "But all voyages show that" "Yes, It's because it's me," I retorted. Realising the dummy had become alive he started to ask questions about my experience, reaching from a nearby shelf I handed him a copy of my book saying "Read all about it". During this pleasant exchange his wife had been admiring the quality of the doeskin cloth and the buttons not tarnished after nearly fifty years, three of them on 'The Briny'. I asked for a 'Please do not touch' sign – can't have strange ladies feeling the width of my cloth. I was pleased with the final outcome (picture 3) the dummy showed my waist line has returned because I now show 6-8" of 'tumble-home' between buttons and button holes when trying it on. There's lots of fun in folk but sometimes one has to dig around a bit to find it.

My contribution to the display introduced me to a local man, 87-year-old submariner, Joe Brighton, who had also provided the museum with artefacts from his navy life, he was in both wars. His survival was a near miracle. I have one of his tapes, which is most enlightening. He did live near Diss, in Scole, near an old Roman Settlement. My faux pas on our meeting was to greet him with the suggestion that our longevity was due to our time on the briny, plenty of ozone, but soon discovered he had breathing difficulties, most probably due to all the years he had spent in the foul atmosphere of submarines. He has loads of pictures etc., but one showing a picture of his submarine H.M. TALLY-HO in February 1944, where a Japanese Corvette in a close encounter, slashed their side ballast tanks with its propellers is something to be seen. They were on the surface at night when they spotted one another and the skirmish began. Much action and they were very, very lucky to manage to limp back in a hell of a state to their base, Trincomalee, Ceylon, some 1200 miles away. Their port side ballast tanks tore open, port hydroplane broken but they saw the Japanese Corvette had beached probably due to loss of manoeuvrability.

Sadly Joe, has now 'Passed over the Bar'.

. . . .

A recent visit to The Potteries, some fifty years after my last visit gave me much food for thought.

With my ten years younger brother Vallance, we visited our old school, Hill Top Boys Elementary School. It had been previously arranged with the Head Mistress, who after welcoming us, introduced us to a lady teacher with a class of children who I guessed were in the 9 to 10 year old category. After introducing us to the class, she then suggested we would like to talk to the children about our time at the school. I was somewhat non-plussed by the request because our visit had been arranged, as we thought, for a conducted tour through the school. Fortunately, the three old school photographs I had with me, I gave to the children to look at and to see whether anyone could recognise me in the groups of fifty classmates, which gave me time to recover my composure.

After a hesitant start I think I was able to claim their interest after describing what it was like during my school days, giving them the opportunity to ask questions. With the help of the teacher and Vallance it became an interesting and enjoyable experience. Needless to say, of the many questions I was asked, two were most pertinent. A boy enquired, "Did I ever fight?" and another "Did I ever have to stand in the corner with a dunce's cap on?" To the former I was able to answer in the affirmative and able to elaborate how fights were arranged after school under fair rules. No bullying, one to one combat with one's 'seconder' holding jackets and in my case my glasses. With regard to the latter question I was able to leave it open, explaining that dunce's caps were not used during my time. On reflection, it would seem the children had 'weighed me up to a tee', a fighter and not very bright. Only one girl identified me in one of the photographs, obviously a girl with a special gift, able to see facial features still remained after seventy plus years.

Some of the rooms were recognisable during the tour, but the internal layout altered to suit the joining of the boys and girls schools. A further change was the absence of male teachers. In my view, I believe men should teach boys, when discipline was emphasised on occasions, with the cane which we responded to with male satisfaction.

After the school visit we wandered around Burslem. The general layout of the town is un-altered but most noticeable were the many open areas where old 'Potbanks' and terraced houses have been demolished most probably necessary due to the modern methods of manufacture and reduced demand. As a teenager, I remember the Wedgwood factory moving out to Barleston, using oil fired kilns, perhaps the beginning of replacing the bottle ovens which used coal for firing the ware during my childhood surrounded by workers small houses.

I was most disappointed however, to miss some fine old buildings, like St. Paul's church at the bottom of Hall Street, the Methodist Chapel at the top (albeit a small part of the façade is left) and the Old Meat Market adjacent to the Town Hall. The latter it would seem being replaced with a modern strange glass skeleton, which may be functional when finished but I cannot imagine it blending in with the stately Town Hall. On reflection the emerging glass skeleton above the hoarding, reminded me of walls topped with broken glass to deter we boys from climbing to investigate what was on the other side.

My most depressing moment was after entering the Wedgwood Institute; I was barred from seeing the classrooms on the first floor where I attended night school, being informed by the librarian that the floors were not safe. Outwardly the building looks fine and will be complemented by the Art School opposite when restoration is complete but in my humble opinion, it is a sacrilege to allow the interior of the Wedgwood Institute to fall into disuse, where Burslem's Arnold Bennett went to school. Further more, any deterioration of the Institute in any form is an insult to the great potter, Josiah Wedgwood. It would seem, from recent research into The Industrial Revolution, that Josiah was a pioneer in mass production long before Henry Ford produced his 'Tin Lizzie' motor car.

106

I must award full marks to the George Hotel, where we stayed, for it's dining room with a pleasant décor enhanced with many pictures of The Potteries of yesteryear, some of which I recall seeing when a small boy. Similarly, after pressing on through the dark forbidding entrance rooms in The Leopard Hotel, to find sanctuary in the tastefully furnished Arnold Bennett Suite.

I'm sure that most of my generation bemoan the fact that today many of the manufactured articles we need are no longer made in Britain. Indeed, when I went to sea, some six thousand British Merchant ships were either part, or fully loaded, with goods made in Britain exported all over the world. Many foreign vessels also called to collect goods made in the United Kingdom. More seriously today there are only about three hundred British manned ships and we depend on foreign vessels bringing goods, fruit etc., for our daily needs.

It is my view that a country must provide food, shelter and energy for it's population, but more importantly today, manufactured goods, a very necessary contribution to maintain and survive in the materialistic motivated world of today.

I noted with pleasure and pride that The Potteries are still providing the world with first class crockery, sanitary ware and ornaments, perhaps not quite on the grand scale of my boyhood years. Nevertheless, it is a heartening feature for the well being of Stoke-on-Trent folk for the future.

So the sooner the Angel or Roman Goddess, either lady would be appropriate, is restored to her rightful place on the top of Burslem's Town Hall, the better, to inspire the natives towards greater endeavour to supply the people's of the world with their famous 'Pots', beautiful ornaments and furniture for their 'comfort stops'!

Here's to the next ride

His and her's

In memoriam to my late dear wife Grace, whose love and caring made my married
life a time never to be forgotton.
The above pictures (September 1998) are dedicated

A POTTERIES LAD

Stanley W. Swain, born in Hall Street, Burslem, Stoke-on-Trent, 1915. Attended Hill Top School and Central Boys' School, Burslem. Studied an Industrial Curriculum continued at night school while he served an apprenticeship in Electrical/Mechanical Engineering, with T. M. Birkett & Sons Brass Founders & Engineers, Hanley, Stoke-on-Trent, Staffordshire.

Eldest of three brothers, spent his formative years in Burslem, with long Summer holidays in Newark-on-Trent, Nottinghamshire.

In 1937 joined The Blue Star Line as an Assistant Engineer Officer, serving in ten steam and motor vessels, and obtained Ministry of Transport, First Class (Chief Engineer Steam & Motorship) Certificate of Competency.

Left the sea in 1949 and took appointment with the British Electricity Authority as a Mechanical Maintenance Engineer, Staythorpe Power Station, Newark-on-Trent. Later joined the South Eastern Region as Specialist Engineer in maintenance problems, retired in 1980.

Now lives in Diss, Norfolk and has one daughter Elaine.

ISBN 0 9523501 1 4